EVERYONE'S IN SALES

Testimonials

I saw Todd Cohen speak at a recent conference and was blown away. His easy-going style and command of the room kept the participants awake, alive, laughing, learning and most importantly . . . ready to sell! I highly recommend Todd for any group of business people who are looking to increase their sales. Which means everyone.

—GENE MARKS, Noted Author, Business Columnist and Speaker

Having worked in a wide variety of management roles over the years in companies big and small, I found Todd's book to be particularly useful in identifying specific ways that companies can successfully create and embed a strong sales-oriented culture. In fact, we have used this line of thinking in my company to great success, even bringing technical developers in line with the need to be "client accountable."

The concept of "sales culture" is what makes this book standout, and it's a concept that far too many companies fail to realize. Todd makes great points that sales requires the entire company, and it means the sales person plays an ever important role as "connector" throughout the company.

—CHUCK SACCO, Founder and CEO, PhindMe Mobile

Todd Cohen is captivating audiences all over the country. He delivers a powerful keynote speech with conviction and humor. He is America's expert on "Sales Culture" and his strategies will take your company's "Sales" to a new level. If you want your profits to soar and your people to produce give him a call today.

—CAROL RITTER, President of Carol Talks
and Philadelphia NSA Chapter President

Everyone's In Sales is wonderful! It opened my eyes that we must leverage our professional networks as part of our personal sales team. *Everyone's In Sales* is equally strong for long-term engaged professionals as well as entrepreneurs. Todd breaks down "Sales" to easy, comfortable, and attainable highly respected goals. He dispels the old sales stereotypes and shifts sales to branding and value proposition."

—ROD COLÓN, AUTHOR OF *Win the Race for 21st Century Jobs*,
HOST OF RADIO SHOW YOUR CAREER IS CALLING,
CAREER COACH AND MOTIVATIONAL SPEAKER

Everyone's in Sales is not only an educational tool for traditional sales teams, but a valuable tool for all areas of an organization. I knew it was going to be my "go to" guide for my internal support teams and for me personally as I transform myself from a Technology Leader to a Business Strategist.

—ANGELO VALLETTA, SENIOR VICE PRESIDENT
AND CHIEF INFORMATION OFFICER, SUN NATIONAL BANK

Todd has proven to be a consummate professional who consistently delivers on his commitments and to the expectations of his clients. His energy and passion for his work is complimented by a positive, uplifting attitude. Todd understands sales and the inherent need for an entire organization to be "engaged" if true success is to be achieved.

—JERRY BLOCK, VICE PRESIDENT, BNYMELLON BANK

I have worked with Todd both in a business and academic setting. He is passionate about helping organizations build a "sales culture" that understands customer needs and develops an out-of-the box approach to the sales process. I have seen him work a room of professionals and get them thinking about the sales process in a whole new way. He is a true sales professional who understands how to build a "value proposition" that really resonates with potential customers. People are inspired by his energy and his passion for the process.

—DR. JEAN WILCOX, PhD PROFESSOR OF MARKETING, TEMPLE UNIVERSITY

The concept of a sales culture that permeates an entire company is so important in today's connected world, and I'm thankful that there are people out there like you who are able to explain not just the personal value, but also the importance to a company's bottom line. Truly, we are all sales people.

—JIM KERR, VICE PRESIDENT OF STRATEGY TRITON MEDIA

Todd's program is WAY more than sales training! Todd instills a mindset and skill set that are far more powerful, meaningful, and lasting. His expertise—building Sales Culture—is about showing sales leaders at companies of all sizes how to multiply their sales effectiveness by harnessing the power of the entire organization and ALL its stakeholders in the pursuit of closing sales. Bigger sales. Better sales. More sales. THAT is the result of implementing Todd's strategies.

—DAVID NEWMAN, PRESIDENT, DO IT! MARKETING

Todd Cohen is first and foremost, an expert in sales: building, managing and motivating sales teams, creating a total sales culture and much more. But he's also a master communicator—engaging and interesting, he weaves humor and his own business experiences into presentations to make them lively, memorable and impactful.

—JAINE LUCAS, EXECUTIVE DIRECTOR,
TEMPLE UNIVERSITY INNOVATION & ENTREPRENEURSHIP INSTITUTE

Now, more than ever, is the time for local broadcasting to embrace your "sales culture" message of *Everyone's in Sales*. Your message to company leaders, "everyone is in sales"—or should be—is a critical call to action that I hope CEO's hear and act on. It may well determine the future of their companies.

—RICHARD V. DUCEY, PhD, CHIEF STRATEGY OFFICER,
PROGRAM DIRECTOR DIGITAL STRATEGIES IN BROADCASTING, BIA/KELSEY

EVERYONE'S IN SALES

How to Unleash
the Power of Sales Culture
to Boost Your Revenues,
Profits and Growth

Todd Cohen

Sales Culture Press LLC

Philadelphia, Pennsylvania

Everyone's in Sales: How to Unleash the Power of Sales Culture
to Boost Your Revenues, Profits and Growth

Published by
Sales Culture Press LLC
Philadelphia, Pennsylvania
866-515-9445

ISBN: 978-0-9828722-1-5 (hardcover)
ISBN: 978-0-9828722-2-2 (softcover)
ISBN: 978-0-9828722-3-9 (Kindle)
ISBN: 978-0-9828722-4-6 (eBook)

Cover and Interior Design and Typesetting:
Desktop Miracles, Inc., Stowe, VT

For information contact:
Todd Cohen
Sales Leader LLC
www.toddcohen.com

For Dad

Who loved me unconditionally and

taught me to be a great sales professional.

Table of Contents

Acknowledgments   11

Introduction   13

CHAPTER 1   Why a Sales Culture?   17

CHAPTER 2   The People of a Sales Culture   27

CHAPTER 3   Building a Foundation for Your Sales Culture   47

CHAPTER 4   Sales Campaigns in a Sales Culture   65

CHAPTER 5   Creating a Sales Culture:
            Expectations and Accountability   81

CHAPTER 6   How Am I Doing?   95

CHAPTER 7   Sales Culture Rides the Trends
            and Bests the Competition   107

CHAPTER 8   A Framework for a Sales Culture:
            How to Build Yours   117

About the Author   141

Book Todd   143

Acknowledgments

When I embarked on this journey, I had no idea how many people would become involved and participate in the process. There are so many people to thank who have provided me with assistance, support, and encouragement along the way. For me, this has been a passage that was meant to be at so many levels.

Thank you to all of the amazing sales professionals I have met and learned from along the way—there are too many of you to mention here, but trust that I know who you all are. To Joel Mickelberg for hiring me right out of school to work at Xerox, and for seeing in me potential I did not yet see in myself. To my friends and colleagues—too numerous to mention—who have listened to me, encouraged me to stay focused and keep writing. Thank you to my editor, Dianne Morr, for the assistance and coaching to help me find my words and craft my thoughts into something interesting.

Thank you to my friend, Michael Hughes, for reading the chapters in various states of completion and for keeping me honest. Thank you to all of my amazing clients for showing faith and belief in me and my vision for a true sales culture.

I hope you enjoy this book—it truly has been a labor of love and it is for you.

TODD COHEN
JULY 2011

Introduction

Dave and Janice are both successful sales professionals selling complex IT products and services. Both have had good long runs of meeting and exceeding quotas and expectations. Both have made very good money and enjoyed all of the kudos and benefits of their success.

But now, things have changed. The economy is bad, clients are pulling back, and business is simply not growing. In short, Dave and Janice are faced with essentially the same dilemma.

They, like you, may be asking these questions:

❏ What can I do to sell differently?

❏ What can I do to develop new and profitable clients?

❑ How can I do a better job ferreting out new opportunities in this economy?

❑ Is there something that I'm missing in my sales toolkit that others are profiting from?

Do some of these questions sound familiar to you?

Face it; we've all read a lot of "quick fix" selling articles that start with "10 Tips" or "The 7 Keys," or "21 Secrets" that promise success selling in a recession. While each starts out well, they all say essentially the same thing with nothing really new.

Let's go back to Dave and Janice. By now, they are probably frustrated and under tremendous pressure to perform. As time drags on both decide to act, but they take very different paths.

Dave continues to make more cold calls, write more proposals, ask more questions, collect more business cards, and send more emails. Now, please note that there is nothing wrong with more activity. Sales is all about meeting your numbers and keeping your activity high, but Dave is going it alone. He is determined to dig out of the slump by himself.

Janice, on the other hand, has begun to create new client relationships by leveraging the skills and passions of all the people around her, both inside and outside her company. She is tapping into ideas from colleagues in the sales department and outside of it, people in customer service, research and development, and marketing. She's working with the accounting department to follow up on big deals from past clients. She's reaching out to her vendor and partner network to see where money is being spent and by whom, to identify promising new prospects. Janice is also keeping her activity high but she is taking a much different view of what it takes to develop and close deals.

In short, Janice is identifying new opportunities through sound sales processes and she is *not* going it alone. Janice is creating and using her **virtual sales team** and creating her own **sales culture.** She has found a way to accelerate her success in these challenging times and set herself up for longer-term stability.

In her sales culture, Janice's team is **virtual** because the members can be in different locations, departments, and/or within different reporting structures. The members don't even have to report to Janice or her manager, but they all share the mission of serving the customer.

Janice supports her team members in their understanding of the art and science of sales so that they are able to support the sales campaign.

Creating a powerful sales culture—an environment where *everyone* is in sales and where the sales process is transparent to the *entire* company—is the vital connection to accelerating your sales results.

Creating a powerful sales culture is the vital connection to accelerating your sales results.

If you think about what it takes to close a deal, it is very much dependent on you, as a sales professional, to harness and leverage the skills and talents of everyone around you—your virtual sales team. This is how people like Janice are raising the bar and seeing increased success. Janice has not just increased her activity; she has learned that a sales campaign is like a movie script needing a powerful cast. Janice is not a one-woman show, but instead the director and choreographer of a cast of talented and skilled people all playing a *selling* role.

She is taking the responsibility to engage and inspire those talented people to be part of her virtual team and to become part of a sales culture. She is proactive, collaborating with her "cast" to help close more and better deals. Janice also figured out one very simple truth. The people around her were all *pleased to be asked* to be a part of solving the sales challenge. Everyone is happy to get more deals in the door, thereby ensuring job security for all. Janice is making her sales culture work for her.

Your job as a selling professional allows you the exciting opportunity to use the networks that you have developed both internally and externally to create and mobilize your virtual sales team. You can get more done and close more deals by engaging those around you. You'll also serve more clients and satisfy more needs. You will generate more referrals and create a sustainable enterprise to grow your business.

What successful sales professionals have figured out is this: If you adopt a sales culture, you'll sell more and sell smarter because you won't ever have to sell by yourself.

1

Why a Sales Culture?

Everyone lives by selling something.
—Robert Louis Stevenson

Welcome to the finest and coolest profession in the world. Sales. Selling. We all do it. You and I and everyone around us.

This book is for everyone because we are all part of a sales culture. It does not matter whether you are in the "C" suite, on the sales team, in the legal department, in human resources, or in marketing. Whether you own a company or are the receptionist for a Fortune 500 company, this is really about you. We are all in sales, including you.

Now given that, let's look at a traditional sales team and the selling profession and consider why sales people are sometimes seen the way they are. In a selling environment without a sales culture, sales teams were sent out to "sell, sell, sell." In many cases, there was no help or support system for them. They were often sent into the world with minimal training and nothing more than a brochure. They had activity metrics to meet and no one else was responsible for them. No one was charged with helping them with a difficult customer issue. They always had to be "on." They could never relax knowing someone "had their back."

They were on their own—to fail or succeed. From this situation, a culture of silos emerged. A siloed management structure is characterized by poor communication and competition rather than cooperation between divisions or departments in a company. Just as the sales professionals were working alone, other colleagues worked in their areas without customer contact. This worked fairly well when products were simple and competition was not so fierce. Sales people had their customers, their long-standing relationships. They did not distract the others in the company with their own needs. Everyone focused on his own job and became very independent.

Sales people also had options to move on to another company or job where they could make more money. And it was entirely possible that the sales people may not have had a strong relationship with others in their company, resulting in less loyalty and satisfaction.

But times have changed and so has the complexity of the sales campaign. People now recognize the need for organizations to rally around the sales effort to provide help, support, and counsel to the sales professionals managing these sales campaigns.

Organizations need to rally around the sales effort to support and counsel the sales professionals managing these sales campaigns.

Today, it is not possible to do business in a silo. Products and the marketplace are too complex. It truly takes a company and all of its members to sell effectively today; it takes a sales culture. Think of the incredible tools we have to sell more efficiently. With the internet, globalization, social media, and unprecedented mobility, customers have access to many vendors and unlimited information.

It truly takes a company and all of its members to sell effectively today; it takes a sales culture.

Problems of a Siloed Culture

Silos of functional areas cause the customer, the #1 priority, to be forgotten. All employees, sales groups and support staff alike, are worrying about their own concerns. The more siloed your organization is, the less likely it is for the sales organization to be successful. For example, in a large manufacturing company, you have people in the organization who are producing goods to fill the customers' orders. If the sales force is talking to the customers and not to the manufacturing folks, the manufacturing staff may never hear the customers' real needs and desires. Without the transfer of this vital information, it is impossible to satisfy customers. How long will customers tolerate this before they find another supplier?

Maximizing the Customer's Voice

A sales culture environment is successful because it maximizes the customer's voice and your service, thereby ensuring satisfaction. This environment puts you in the best place to serve customers and close as many sales as possible. The customer comes first. Sales organizations are empowered and energized to create a solution for the client. The company is behind you to support the collective interests of the customer and the company. In a customer-centered culture, everybody is exploring ways to satisfy the customer all the time.

A good sales professional understands the abilities and constraints of the members of the virtual team.

In a company with a sales culture, better internal communication puts the sales organization in a better position to accurately represent what the company can build and deliver. Both sales and production people must hear the voice of the customer in order to cost-effectively deliver on customer needs. A well-developed sales culture is the key to success.

Here is another key point in understanding sales culture: Everyone involved in a sale makes up a virtual team. The virtual team includes every person who contributes to the success of the sales campaign being managed by the sales professional. Everyone on the virtual team collaborates willingly to create a common effort to meet the customer's needs. Virtual teams are unlimited in their efforts and value to the sales culture environment.

Advantages of a Sales Culture

In a sales culture you and your virtual team all begin to embrace what the customer is thinking. You have the exciting opportunity to become a customer advocate to other experts in your company. You become the "go to" person who can deliver results, because you have a sales culture to work with. The silos break down and everyone understands the sales organization and the selling role.

It is exciting when everyone in an organization begins to understand his role in the company's big picture and in the sales cycle and process.

The sales team, in turn, understands the abilities and constraints of the other people in the company. It is exciting when everyone in an organization begins to understand his role in the company's big picture and in the sales cycle and process. A sales culture has been born and good outcomes result.

Everyone understands the customer's needs. They are all working together. Everyone negotiates, both internally and externally. In a sales culture, everyone seeks "to understand, then to be understood," as Stephen Covey put it.

My First Model for a Sales Culture

While the term sales culture may sound new, the concept is not. I began learning about a sales culture in my childhood. I watched my father, my first sales hero, take wedding photographs throughout my youth. My father was selling more than his photos. He was selling his services to provide a remembrance of the day and was, of course, selling himself.

He was an artist, not only because he took beautiful pictures, but because he really understood and related to the people in the photos. My father was very well-respected and he made a nice living taking and selling his photos. His customers were always delighted and referred him to all their friends and acquaintances. He was a genuine person. He was passionate about his work and his customer's pictures. He, the bride, the groom, and their families would talk at length about just the right light, angle, setting, and scenes to be included. He never considered their requests to be a burden. He wanted them to remember their day as "perfect." The pictures had to be the best they could be.

Dad created a sales culture and a virtual team of those who helped to make the pictures perfect. His suppliers, his developers and his studio helpers all understood the needs of the customer and the value of the photographs to the customer. Dad was always about quality, but mostly he was about people. He was never without work. There was always another wedding to shoot.

---

*Dad was about quality, but mostly
he was about people.*

Not surprisingly, my part-time jobs as a teenager always involved sales. There was the job in the Bonanza Steakhouse kitchen. My customers were the order takers, the diners out for an evening, and the owners of the Steakhouse. They all had equal priority in my mind as I sought to serve them.

Then there was the retail jewelry store, where young couples were looking for engagement and wedding rings, and finally the clothing store where young men like myself were looking for their first job interview suits. I learned from my father that the buying customer had needs beyond the actual purchase. They needed to feel good about their purchase.

Sales Culture in the Corporate Environment

When I started my post-college career, I wanted to create Dad's type of relationships and help people with their needs as a reliable sales person. Xerox invited me to enter their renowned sales training program. I wasn't really sure how to become a super sales person, but this company had a great reputation, was very successful, and allowed me to learn.

In retrospect, I think the attraction between Xerox and me was the shared conviction that the customer was most important. The sales process was not about making the sale as much as about making the customer happy and satisfied. This was my concept of selling, based on my earliest memories of my father and his photographs. It was also the way this company had found success by relating to its customers.

The sales process was not about making the sale as much as about making the customer happy and satisfied.

From my earliest days with the company, I embraced their sales model. This model, simply stated, is that the customer comes first. The customer pays our bills. He pays our salaries. Everything was done for the benefit of the customer.

Ultimately, the company culture established that the sales organization led the way for all. It was the eyes and ears of the company. The sales organization then was empowered to engage our internal company resources. These internal experts were encouraged to work with sales professionals in this way.

The Sales Professional

The sales professional is the key to creating a sales culture for best customer results. The sales professionals are well trained, motivated, and compensated within a sales organization that is empowered and encouraged to interact and build a virtual team across the organization. Keep in mind that while the sales professional is in an excellent position to start creating a sales culture, anyone in any role in a company can take the lead to create a sales culture.

The sales professional does not make the sale "no matter what." He is interested in building the virtual team, in doing things better for the customer and, ultimately, for the company. This is not a "compensation" mentality, rather an innate knowledge of how to inspire and influence the members of the virtual team to deliver for the company.

In my sales career, I have established several long-standing relationships with some sales "greats." I still communicate with these folks and recall their excellence often. They are mentors, always guiding me in my sales approach. This book is about sharing their messages and their greatness with you. The ***sales career*** is about the customer, not about the sales person, his quota, his territory, or even his compensation. When selling is about the customer, everyone wins.

This book provides a guide to building a sales culture. It also shares the wisdom of the people who have established, lived, and thrived in exceptional sales cultures along the way.

The Elements of a Sales Culture

A sales culture is easy to create, once you understand the critical elements and how they work together. You will learn these elements and their inner-workings in the following chapters of this book.

Chapter 2 describes the characteristics of the people who make up a sales culture. Their personal and relational skills and their business acumen are described in detail. We introduce the concept and the importance of Relationship Portability. We also include a description of how the skills of all the people in a sales culture can be used to leverage valuable internal and external customer relationships.

Chapter 3 includes a methodology for leveraging the sales culture skills. Using these skills to create a solid sales culture involves building a virtual team of subject-matter experts who can satisfy all aspects of customer needs. This virtual team is led by members of the sales organization.

Chapter 4 reviews the sales cycle as it touches all organization members. Sales culture thinking will help the sales professionals integrate the expertise of all organization members into the virtual team, to help support and sustain the sales process, to close sales, and to maintain company revenue levels.

Chapter 5 describes how all organization members must be directed by understanding that they are part of a sales culture. Sales leadership must create the expectation that the sales professionals will engage others in the organization and provide direction on how to contribute effectively to each sales cycle. Other leaders in the organization must also create the environment that encourages participation and contribution of needed expertise. These other leaders include the CEO and other executive managers.

Chapter 6 describes the collaboration that happens when the customer is a partner to the sales cycle and in the innovation initiatives of the company. The sales professional acknowledges the customer's role in the sales culture by seeking feedback on his own performance. When customers are integrated into research and planning, there is significant sustainability built in. A sales culture provides the structure that supports these relationships.

Chapter 7 provides the formula for creating value by leveraging current trends and understanding the competition. It also explains how to leverage the power of the sales culture to create new and sustainable value.

And finally, **Chapter 8** includes "how to" recommendations and explains how to implement a sales culture environment in your organization.

2

The People of a Sales Culture

*For every sale you miss because you are too
enthusiastic, you will miss a hundred because you
are not enthusiastic enough.*

—Zig Ziglar

The people of a sales culture are not just sales people. Interesting concept. So who are these people? You will be surprised. The people of a sales culture include all the organizational members who practice what I have defined as the essential selling skills of great sales professionals. Those skills are:

❑ Strong personal skills

❑ Strong relational skills

❑ Excellent business acumen

When I present workshops and training to prepare professionals to grow in a sales culture, we include many people who don't have "sales" in their job title. Some people are surprised to learn they have a role in the sales culture and that they can develop their skills to make a greater contribution to their organization's success.

Personal, relational, and business skills allow all the people of the sales culture to work together to create and leverage customer relationships. Most important, though, is the recognition that these customer relationships all depend on internal employee relationships. We all sell. The sales culture appears.

Personal Skills

Personal skills are seen in the way you present yourself and the things you naturally do well. Early in my career, I worked with people at Xerox and at a few dot coms who had an obvious and innate gift that allowed them to sell. They *liked* to sell. It was apparent, and it was amazing and exhilarating to watch. The essential selling skills came naturally to them as an extension of who they were. These people were selling in each conversation, each interaction, and each exchange of information.

Everyone in your company can develop essential selling skills and this chapter tells you how. The desire to sell can be developed as people work together to understand and serve the customer. The desire to sell is important, but it is supported by other personal skills of passion, energy, self-motivation, and integrity.

SALES PROFESSIONAL STORY

David, a dot com co-founder, was a great sales guy. He had the most incredible self-motivation of all of the great sales people I have encountered.

David had a brilliant business mind and the know-how to start a business. David was among the first to create a new vision for MBA level education. He saw that he could facilitate the delivery of Ivy League quality graduate education to busy executives through online e-courses. He established a company to present that offering, and sold the concept enthusiastically and effectively. He was passionate about the value of new e-learning MBA level courses presented by highly qualified professors. His passion enhanced his selling skills. David's spirit was contagious and soon all the members of the sales staff were incredibly motivated to sell.

David's energy conveyed how these courses could make people's lives better, tremendously helping busy executives become more effective. He engaged professors from top universities, met with clients, and inspired passion in everyone. Most importantly, he inspired the members of his own organization. His incredible self-motivation, passion, genuine concern, and integrity touched the client. David would weave together a unique solution for each client; they experienced his vigor and intensity. At the same time, David modeled for his sales people an innate desire and ability to sell.

His sincere approach was perceived as an effort to educate, share, and communicate a passion for something wonderful. To the client, it didn't even seem like he was selling. His integrity was unquestioned as he transparently followed through on all elements of the agreement.

One day David visited a potential customer. His passion about the new MBA courses conveyed a sense of the unique value to the customer. Even though the customer had no budget for purchasing these courses, David and the customer negotiated a plan to use the courses in a way that added value to the customer and revenue for David's company. Payment terms were creative and both parties benefited.

The plan David devised was to provide "train-the-trainer" services for the customer, enabling the customer to use the course materials. David's payment would be a small percentage of all new sales resulting from the training. As the customer's business expanded, David received recurring revenue. Both parties were happy and continued along a path to growth and success. David believed strongly and passionately in his value proposition and services, he knew that his offering would yield a great return for his customer. He was able to convince the customer to take a chance and, ultimately, share revenue with him. This is an example of the personal skills that every successful sales person needs in order to be a part of and/or lead a sales culture.

Relational Skills

We all know that people like to do business with people, not with an impersonal "organization." People are motivated to buy as much by your knowledge as by your ability to understand and sympathize with their plight. This is where your relational skills come into play. Your relational skills result from applying your personal skills to build solid relationships. Your skills foster productive relationships with customers and also internal relationships that create and foster the sales culture in your organization. Strong relational skills allow both your clients and colleagues to trust you to "do right by them."

So what are the skills needed to create and sustain great relationships? They start with the qualities of humility, ego control, confidence, and personal responsibility. Upon this base you can build the skills of collaboration, listening, and patience. This is a winning formula for building successful relationships.

Your clients and colleagues trust
you to "do right by them."

SALES PROFESSIONAL STORY

Karen, one of the sales managers at Xerox, showed exceptional ability to create the right kind of relationships, both with clients and with internal staff people. She was a very confident and poised person and completely focused on one thing—understanding her clients and making them feel important. She always knew what she was about. Karen's ego was never out of control; her listening skills were amazing and worked wonders for her. Karen was the best sales manager I ever had.

She was never too rushed to listen and to listen carefully. She let me and the client know that she was listening. She didn't interrupt, but interjected a word of understanding or support at just the right time. She exhibited exceptional patience even if what the client was talking about seemed irrelevant on the surface. She was so amazing at this that no one really picked up on her technique or knew that she was doing it consciously. She just made everyone feel tended, including the sales people she was responsible to manage. She was kind and effective in her coordination.

The result? As I developed as a sales professional under her tutelage, I emulated her listening skills. As a team, we sold more consistently because she encouraged us to use relationship skills as she used them with us and with the clients. Collaboration was something that happened because she practiced collaboration with us as well as with the client. We understood that.

As a result of Karen's efforts we truly felt that we were "all in it together." She brought out *our* confidence and we all helped each other. We all held her (and each other) to a high level of responsibility and esteem because she held herself to the highest level of personal responsibility and esteem. We created our sales culture because of Karen's way of doing business.

As a result of Karen's efforts we truly felt that we were "all in it together."

Let me give you another example of Karen's effect on my sales success. On a particular sales call that Karen and I made together, the potential customer was in a hurry, preoccupied with something, and not really listening to us. Karen mentioned to the customer that perhaps there was a better time to talk about this, as we didn't want to intrude on his busy, demanding schedule. She commented in a very compassionate way that she recognized his inattentive mode. That reminded the customer that he had invited us to discuss his needs for a new product that Karen and I were selling. Karen then asked to briefly and succinctly summarize the value proposition of our new product. The conversation continued and we actually started down the discovery path to helping this customer.

Karen navigated this difficult task, and then confidently introduced me to continue the conversation. She was not along on the call for her own glory or success, but to do her part as a member of my virtual team to support a sale.

The other aspect of the sales culture that Karen demonstrated is the balance between confidence and humility. Karen knew that sales people must be confident, and at the same time must also be humble and patient. It is their humility and patience that enable them to listen intently, to truly understand the value that a colleague or client brings to the discussion. She had humbly observed that another time might be better for the customer, making the importance of our call secondary to the customer's need at the moment.

The balance between confidence and humility is an important aspect of the sales culture.

If you don't have humility and great patience for those around you, customers and colleagues will not be part of your trusted or trusting circle. They will not be part of your virtual team. No matter how sharp you may be, it is almost impossible to be successful if you don't have others helping you. In a nutshell, better listening really allows you to develop and benefit from all of the other relational skills needed to be a great sales person.

Do You Have RP?

How strong are your business relationships? Do your business relationships extend beyond the sales transactions you complete every day? If you changed careers would you ever hear from those people in your database again?

The real question is this:
Do you have RP—Relationship Portability™?

RP is a key differentiating factor that separates sales reps from great sales professionals. A strong sales culture is made of sales professionals who have the ability to cultivate long term relationships and continually build on them. A sales professional with great relationship portability knows that those relationships will stay with him or her as careers and jobs change over time.

In any business climate, good or bad, change is inevitable. Products evolve, become obsolete, and are replaced by newer, better products. Sometimes companies go out of business, are bought out, or merge. You may be offered new opportunities. When all these changes happen, the strongest asset you have is your RP.

SALES PROFESSIONAL STORY

Sales professional Jim sold paper to companies in a large metropolitan area. Even though we keep hearing promises of becoming a paperless society, it hasn't happened yet. So someone has to fill the need for all the paper that cranks through printers and gets turned into business letters, direct marketing mailers, and award certificates. That was Jim—until a colleague offered him a position in the sales department of his specialized software development company.

Jim had a great relationship portability index (RPi). His relationships went far beyond just filling his customers' need for paper. He had become part of his customers' virtual teams. He anticipated their needs. He talked with them about the evolution of their businesses. He was an honest sounding-board about the changes in the marketplace. He referred business to them and introduced them to other professionals in his network.

When Jim needed to start making connections to learn about companies' software needs, he didn't have to make cold calls. With his high RPi, Jim could call the people who had bought paper from him.

If you have a decent business relationship with a paper buyer, he or she can probably give you the name of a colleague who is in a position to buy customized software. Because Jim has a great RPi, his customers were willing to go far beyond that. They would call a buddy in the right department and introduce Jim. They would say, "If you need anything, just call Jim. He'll take good care of you."

They would tell Jim about someone from their Rotary or Lions club who might need software. They kept in touch with Jim as their careers changed as well.

Increase Your RPi

If you have a great RPi, your network and your virtual team grows and grows. Another way to think of this is: Your relationships are "platform neutral."

The ultimate question is: Can you leverage your existing relationships to act as a part of your virtual sales team? Can they be part of your virtual team even if they do not have the ability or need to buy from you as they have done in the past?

What is your relationship portability index or your RPi? Try this exercise. Make a list of all of your business relationships.

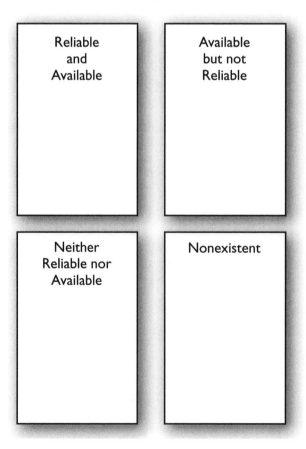

Reliable and Available	Available but not Reliable
Neither Reliable nor Available	Nonexistent

Then rate them this way:

- **Reliable and Available.** They will always refer you and believe in you as a selling professional. They will make it a priority to introduce you to people in their organization without question. They are consistently available to you and are strong advocates for you as a sales professional and as a business professional.

- **Available but not Reliable.** They are available and will take your call and refer you, but not without some concern. They are not consistently reliable to be a part of your virtual team. Personal trust may be an issue.

- **Neither Reliable nor Available.** They don't see you as a part of their business and are not at all extendable.

- **Nonexistent.** These are people you know—maybe from a community organization or your social group—that you have never thought of as a possible business associate. These are RP possibilities waiting to happen. Nonexistent can also mean "not yet."

A sales culture is powered by the virtual team and, by extension, your RPi. The virtual team is powered by your RPi. Make no mistake—if you can transport and leverage your business relationships with you throughout your professional career, you have a high degree of RP and the potential to be more successful is obvious. If not, you will become stuck as you change and grow and find yourself starting over often.

SALES PROFESSIONAL STORY

My father, Marvin Cohen, understood the need to relate, and that is why he was never without delighted customers who were happy to refer others to him. He not only related well to his customers, but to his virtual team as well. His RPi was very good.

One day his film supplier was low on the film that Dad needed. The vendor only stocked a limited amount and did not have the quantity that dad would need in the next two weeks. Dad knew that he would need lots of this film, so he ordered a six-month supply of the film paying for it in advance. With cash in hand, his supplier was able to stock more film, and also help my Dad with his need. Dad didn't want to find another supplier, as he had a trusting relationship with this one. Why not help each other solve a short-term problem? All went well. Dad and this supplier continued to help each other in many ways beyond the customer-supplier relationship for many years after this incident.

Learning at Dad's Side

I was able to learn great lessons from Dad because he brought me along on sales calls. Later in my life and especially in the years that my father has been gone, I realized that he was building his relationship with me by demonstrating the qualities and skills I would need to be successful in life. We had fun together as he shared his passion for what he did. He built our relationship using more of that same unique talent to understand and relate to people for lasting relational value. I always felt honored to be a part of his "team." I realized my father was giving me a gift, one that he was uniquely capable of bestowing on his son.

Business Acumen Skills

Once the first essential skills of a sales culture, personal and relational skills, are established—what then? How do you get a signed contract?

To truly answer this question, you must address yourself to yet another set of skills: business acumen. Business acumen is absolutely essential for turning a relationship into a business initiative. Business acumen skills include an awareness of the total business environment and condition of your company, the ability to create a business plan with required activities for your clients, understanding how to be competitive, and making sure that you ask for the order. These skills are essential to managing the sales cycle, but even more importantly, to managing the others in your organization who will help you close sales.

The people who help you close sales are the members of your virtual team. You have built relationships with them to help you support the diverse needs of your customer before, during, and after the close of a sales campaign. This is a sales culture at work and you are the sales professionals in charge to make it work for the client.

Understanding your company's business needs, as well as the needs of the subject-matter experts on your virtual team, is essential in order to meet your clients' needs. Business leaders, sales leaders, and sales people each have a business plan. They come from different perspectives, but each has a plan and each has goals to meet.

Sales professionals and leaders run businesses. The greatest sales professionals understand this and exercise great business acumen to grow their business. They regard themselves as the CEOs of their sales territories. They see their territories as providing a series of opportunities to make good business decisions. They have the courage to walk away from bad business—business that clearly wastes the virtual team's time and expertise—and the courage to chase good business, even when difficulties and obstacles interfere. That is solid business acumen—the ability to decide what is good business and what isn't.

Sales professionals regard themselves
as the CEO of their sales territory.

Developing business acumen, to understand where your business plan supports and relates to the business and sales leader's plans, is essential to a successful sales professional. Let's explore how you develop and use these skills within a sales culture.

SALES PROFESSIONAL STORY

Ralph had well-developed business acumen and perspective. He was extremely analytical and competent, understanding and evaluating all business angles for best results. He truly saw the "big picture" when it came to his territory and the company's overarching plan. His territory consistently produced more business through coherent, researched, and well-thought-out decisions.

Once or twice Ralph had to end a relationship with a customer. The customer was not willing to share in the essential conversation and planning process that would lead to his own satisfaction. The sales effort was clearly not going to bring satisfaction to either the customer or to Ralph's company. These indications were well-documented and considered, and made great business sense.

With years of experience considering business cases, Ralph could analyze costs and benefits quickly. He was very intuitive and always knew what was in his and the company's best interest, and he acted upon that intuition. He was not afraid to ask for clarity when he was not sure of his customer's intentions. He knew how to be competitive, both from an external as well as an internal cost perspective. Ralph thought in business terms, not only in sales terms.

On one occasion that I remember, Ralph seemed to be having trouble with a complex and challenging sale. The customer obviously needed the product, but wasn't moving toward agreement. Ralph continued to go back time and again to seek more clarity on needs, extending the questioning or discovery aspect of this multi-tiered and complex relationship. Ultimately, Ralph and his virtual team were able to win the deal. He never let the conversation focus on price or on a competitor's lesser value. He continued to seek value for the customer and for his company.

Finding value became the focus of Ralph's endeavors and the customer came to appreciate this approach and the potential value that it brought to both parties. As it turned out, the customer needed a unique customization to an existing product that would require research and development investment. Ralph used his business acumen and saw that this customization and expenditure could be a good thing for his company and that this was good for business. Other customers could benefit from the customization as well. This is the way new markets are created.

Business acumen skills give you the ability to identify and negotiate a better solution that is a win-win. Stepping back, looking for the elements of a solution, doing more discovery with the client, and making a better value proposition for both of you are examples of solid business acumen. Success is achieved when everyone is satisfied with the result. Everyone must like the result. That is the win-win. The foresight to make strong business decisions is imperative.

$$\text{Customer's Needs} + \text{New Products and Services} = \text{Money in the Bank}$$

Leveraging Relationships with Your Customers

We all know that satisfied customers breed other customers. Another thing they do for you is to help you design your new products and services. When several people in your organization have relationships with your customers, your colleagues are able to glean valuable information by conversing with customers, providing services, and gaining a solid understanding of how those customers are expanding their businesses. This gives you greater insight on how you can continue to serve that customer with your evolving products and services. As you recognize what their needs will be in the future, you can plan your products and services accordingly. These relationships are like "money in the bank."

Sales professionals who lead the way for others in your organization to develop these relationships are invaluable. They lead their virtual teams to create great value.

In Conclusion

Selling is not simple today and it is getting more complex every day. It takes the generous efforts of many people to sell in current markets. Individual efforts are both empowering and important. The job of the sales professional is to help individuals on the virtual team in the sales culture to use their talents and expertise to serve the customer, satisfying needs as they arise. The sales professional has the right and responsibility to lead others to work as a team, using selling skills as they apply to each person's expertise.

This is a new era in sales and for you as a sales professional. This is the era of the sales culture which is supported and thrives by the collective actions of the virtual team. Everyone is truly in sales, and this presumes a new role for the sales professional. The sales professional must find and enable the leader in each member of the organization; they no longer solely own the customer; they own the sales campaign and the responsibility to develop the business. This means lots of other members of the virtual team have a wonderful and satisfying opportunity to infuse and integrate their expertise to satisfy the customer.

The sales professional must find and enable the leader in all members of the organization.

Helping people to develop sales skills and leverage them into customer relationships is not only invaluable to the company, it is essential for success in current economy.

If you like to work alone, and are resistant to collaboration and joint efforts, you will find it hard to work within a sales culture environment. If, on the other hand, you like people and sharing work values, you will benefit from this environment. You will find you have more confidence in yourself, your company, its products and services, and, finally, your ability to deliver unequivocal value to your customer.

My sales heroes have paved the way for sales professionals today. I have encountered so many heroes in my career and I am happy to share their inspiration in this book. They are artists and their art must be understood in the context of what we must accomplish as sales professionals. These heroes and their stories help unfold the concept of a sales culture throughout the rest of this book.

Questions for you to think about

1. Do you consider yourself a sales professional?

2. Why? Why not?

3. What you do contributes to your company's bottom line. What skills can you improve to be more effective?

4. Can you say that you have a great relationship with your clients or customers? Or do they buy from you only because they need your product?

5. Do you consider yourself a business professional?

6. Do you have a business plan for your territory?

7. Do you listen more than you talk?

8. Do you know when to ask for the order and how to ask for the order?

9. Are your running a business or existing in one?

3

Building a Foundation for Your Sales Culture

You get out front and you stay out front.

—A.J. Foyt

You now know about the personal and relational skills and the competencies required for an effective sales culture, but that's just the start. As essential as these skills are, they must be integrated and aligned to leverage them into a solid sales culture. You continue to create your sales culture by building your virtual team of subject-matter experts who can satisfy all aspects of customer needs. Building your virtual team involves a lot of trust and significant investments in your relationship building. We rely on the sales professional to lead the virtual team, but it takes the knowledge, skills, and vision of all the team members to win the business.

Linking Skills to Sales to Create a Sales Culture

Sales professionals often know intuitively that they need to create a network of their internal and external colleagues in order to tap all the skills needed to serve the customer. These personal and relational skills need to be inherent to the members of the sales organization to create the sales culture effectively. This is another way of saying that you maintain your relationship portability. If you maintain your RPi, and help those around you develop their personal and relational skills, then you are creating your own sales culture.

Try this simple exercise. Sit down, think through your process of preparing and working with a customer, and then create a mind map or flowchart of that process. Add to the map the names of people who are included in this process. What does each contribute? How do you connect to each? List others who should be connected and how and what each will need to contribute.

It is important to think about the virtual team as a dynamic, fluid, ever-changing entity. There may be some individuals who are always on your team—maybe a supplier or an administrative assistant. Other roles depend on the opportunity that the campaign addresses or the phase of the sales cycle. For example, you may need a product developer on your team when you are learning how to satisfy your client's needs. Later you may need a technician to install or trouble-shoot the product during the delivery phase. Finally, customer support personnel might play an important role on your team to assist the client using the product after the sale is complete.

Your virtual team is a dynamic,
fluid, ever-changing entity.

Ask yourself how you will leverage the skills of these contributors, inspire and motivate them, contact them, and make sure they are in the flow of the customer interactions. What other individual connections, group connections, email contacts, and so on should you include in your virtual team?

Other considerations include how you will communicate with your team beyond email, such as conference calls, regularly scheduled sessions, follow-up emails, and invitations to be a part of a sales call. Can you do it? How can you engage, empower, and enable them to participate? For you to build your virtual team you need to be able to answer these questions and, in time, creating your virtual team becomes second nature.

Think about how we have defined sales culture. "Everyone is in sales!" If you believe that everyone is in sales, your job is to help others understand this, too, and to contribute in effective ways to your customers and their satisfaction.

Your job is to help your colleagues recognize their skills, strengthen them, and use them as part of your virtual team.

The key is to make sales thinking second nature in your virtual team members. Does this sound tricky or hard to you? It's not and I am going to tell you why. While sales thinking may not be as natural to some as to others, we all have some reasonable sales instincts that carry us through. Everyone has to do some sort of selling all the time. You no doubt used some sales skills to get hired for your job. That is an example of the sales ability people use every day.

As the sales leader, you have an amazing opportunity to bring out those sales instincts in people and show them how to help the sales campaign. You become a powerful coach and mentor to your colleagues. Once someone becomes a member of a virtual team, they are accountable to the team and free to act on behalf of the team.

SALES PROFESSIONAL STORY

I have seen sales professionals bring out the sales instincts in many virtual teams. One specific and significant incident takes me back to my sales professional friend, Karen. Through a "grapevine" connection at Xerox, we found out late in the game that we had not been included in a national bid for a large utility contract. We were apparently locked out and no one let us know about the bid, despite a small presence at the account. As Karen thought that the opportunity must not be lost, she called on the utility, found the person responsible for bid acceptance, and began to develop a relationship.

Karen's task was not easy and she had an uphill battle. She successfully noted our previous work with the utility company, our sincere interest in serving their needs, our ability to customize to their specific value concepts, and so forth. In short order, Karen convinced her contact to let us bid.

Having secured the request for a proposal, Karen had to win enthusiastic engagement in the bid process back at the office. At Xerox, people were feeling offended and disappointed at initially being left out. The stakes were high, indeed. And we had an internal and external battle to wage to get everyone aligned to compete for this business.

To this day, I will never forget how Karen walked from cubical to cubical talking to all those who needed to be included. She was carefully and deliberately building her virtual team. Karen had assigned sales professional Candice to lead the team, so she took Candice with her to hear her pitch as she invited each person to be a part of the team. Candice then took the lead engaging the virtual team—the services group, contracts personnel, technical staff and experts, and another sales person—in a meeting focused on responding to the utility company's request for a proposal.

Our time was short and the virtual team would have to come together very quickly, understand the utility's needs and environment, and of course, the Xerox environment and capabilities. One hundred percent participation would be required. It was all or nothing. The *all* was huge and the *nothing* would be painful! Everyone needed to have a very high sense of urgency. No interruptions or distractions, electronic or otherwise, could be tolerated. The team members needed to dedicate their time completely to this endeavor. Candice asked people to replace themselves if they could not fulfill this level of commitment. This project of preparing our bid had to take priority over all else for the next two weeks. This piece of business was large enough to warrant undivided attention.

Each member of the virtual team was, in fact, a subject-matter expert who owned a defined role. Candice explored the client's business needs and assigned each team member a set of tasks depending on the member's strengths. For the virtual team to succeed, each member needed to understand everyone's assignments and how they aligned. It was an intense and complicated process. It was exciting, as well, to see a team coalesce and develop a rhythm. Karen managed many other areas so she gradually moved on to another project, leaving Candice to manage this process, only checking in briefly every few days.

It is exciting to see a team coalesce and develop a rhythm and create their own sales culture.

Perhaps originally being left out of the bidding actually sparked our serious interest in making our bid a win-win. We worked intensely in our bid preparation. Everyone did what was necessary, and then some, to create our best impression and competitive bid. Learning about others' needs and work was continuous. We became a virtual team with a mission. We were not going to lose this bid!

Karen inspired this effort for the sales professional and for the virtual team by engaging us all to invest our personal and relational skills to not only prepare but to *win* the bid. At the end of two weeks we submitted the winning bid. It was a work of art and beauty.

The Sales Culture Maintains and Sustains Skills

Now let's discuss how the sales culture environment can actually maintain and sustain the essential skills necessary for success. Once the sales culture is created, it can build momentum towards a company culture in which everyone believes and embraces the concept that everyone is in sales, and actually has fun with it. I have seen many a sales professional motivate the "non-sales professional" to get involved simply by demonstrating their passion and client commitment.

When everyone in the company believes that everyone is in sales, it is easy to see that no one works alone. Obviously, no individual can solve a customer's problem or provide products and services alone. Everyone needs to understand the customer's needs in order to integrate the work required to satisfy those needs. In a sales culture environment, people help each other make individual contributions to satisfy the customer's needs.

*An individual cannot provide
products and services alone.*

If a company does not have a sales culture, the reason may be that leaders have not figured out how to draw people out of their silos. When competent people are able to work across groups, you begin to create the environment in which everyone understands his part in bringing sales home. Motivating, rewarding, and inspiring people to work with others are key actions to create a sales culture. When everyone has a concept of being in sales and the sales organization can minimize attention to internal politics, virtual sales teams can invest their energy on the external customer.

Company leaders, as well as sales leaders, must commit to motivating and inspiring people to work on a team. Building a virtual team can take minutes or months, depending on how effective the leadership of a company is in bringing people together to become a customer-centric sales culture.

Most times people agree to work on a virtual team just because they are asked. Of course, people have the option of declining if they are already over-committed or don't feel the fit is right, but in a vibrant sales culture, serving on virtual teams becomes the norm.

Leaders can share information quite easily, and in a sales culture they do just that. I have seen the most effective sales cultures thrive because the top echelon considered themselves the Chief Sales Officers. It is then up to the individuals in the organization to determine how they can best work to further achieve team goals. When all agree intellectually, we all strive for results, profits, and immediate quarterly numbers.

A virtual team can be built in minutes or months, depending on the leadership.

Cooperation Leads to Strong Teams

The sales professional in a company is specifically responsible for understanding the needs of the client and transferring those needs to the virtual team. An example of this teamwork is seen when a sales representative shares his perspective on how to close the deal with a Human Resources (HR) person.

The sales leader needs to build a virtual sales team. HR supports the sales campaign by writing job descriptions that reflect the sales skills needed in all the virtual team member's roles. It is the responsibility of HR and the virtual team leader to communicate clearly and succinctly the needed job responsibilities, skills, and aptitudes. That way the company is able to hire people who fit the business and the prevalent sales culture. Then the sales culture is more likely to succeed and ensure that sales campaigns are effective.

The sales professional and HR work
together to enhance the sales culture
by hiring the right people.

Sales professionals help others, in this case an HR specialist, to put on a business hat and see the bigger picture. The HR colleague, in turn, helps sales leaders, professionals, and reps see the limitations of what is possible and realistic. In a sales culture, the two groups are working together to create a sales organization set up to succeed and prosper.

SALES PROFESSIONAL STORY

As sales professional David was developing his start-up business, selling e-learning MBA level courses, he was very focused on the customer. As he added employees, they were also focused on the customer and his needs. But this focus got diluted as the company grew. New employees were more focused on their individual areas because there was so much demand for their work. They didn't seem to have time to consider what others were doing.

David realized that, for the company to grow, he had a challenge. He needed the additional employees since his business was successful, but he hadn't taken the time to make them part of the team. They were all expert at what they did, but they didn't really understand the business and the customers.

Trouble was brewing. One customer felt as if he was not being served and cut his order in half, deciding to try another vendor. This customer really needed to depend on his vendors and, since David's company didn't have the personalized service that it once did, the customer felt the need to look for security elsewhere.

After David lost two other long-term customers because of poorer customer service than they had been accustomed to, he decided to restore the sales culture that his customers remembered. David successfully addressed the problem and revived the sales culture because he instilled into the company his mantra "We are all in sales." This took time and people had to be convinced that they could participate without repercussions.

The sales culture again focused on the client's needs. In time his company gained the lost customers back by restoring the necessary sales culture. People started to have a better understanding of what they would be expected to do and why it served the company for them to do it. The sales campaigns took on a new meaning and all turned out well for David and his company. David was now back to his original culture that had initially made him a success with his customers.

An Effective Virtual Team and Sales Culture

I see examples of effective virtual teams and sales cultures everywhere I go. I see many examples, but still not enough to indicate that sales culture practices are commonplace and clearly understood by sales organizations. When the sales professionals thoroughly understand what they have to do and know how to engage people, the organizational managers say, "Yes! Go to work and be on the team." No distractions on competing priorities are presented by different levels of functional bosses.

Sales professionals can help set priorities by always keeping the needs of the client as the primary focus.

The virtual team members' biggest challenge might be time management. The balancing of functional responsibilities and virtual team responsibilities to the customer can be tricky. One way to bring clarity to this challenge is to think of the customer and his needs first. What will help to satisfy the customer? How urgent is the customer's need for my service? What works best for the customer? How can I help to move the sales campaign to a successful close?

Functional managers and sales professionals who are leading the virtual teams can help team members prioritize their work in ways that contribute to customer satisfaction and company success. Whatever affects a customer comes first.

Organizational managers can look at activities in two categories: customer issues and internal issues. If the environment or culture of the company is one that prioritizes the customer before all else, then everyone knows how to manage their time according to these guidelines. The internal issues need to be managed to best respond to the customer issues.

As a sales professional you can see every situation as a unique opportunity to reinforce a sales culture. Each sales opportunity may offer a different investment in your emotional bank account. This account is built by developing relationships with customers and virtual team members who can contribute to customer relationships.

Serving Both Current and New Customers

Sales professionals must align the needs of new and current customers. They are responsible for all parties involved and engaging them as needed to serve both sets of customers.

Do sales professionals move on after the sales campaign is won? The answer is no! The greatest sales professionals are actually still involved after the campaign and this should be the standard. They continue to foster the customer relationships and acknowledge and reward all contributors. And when the deal is sent "over the fence" to be fulfilled, they continue to monitor the relationships that were developed to get the deal closed. The relationships made the deal happen. So the relationships need to be maintained and nurtured to keep your RPi high.

The effective sales professional takes the time and makes the effort to *acknowledge* the virtual team members' contributions, sincerely *thank* them, and *ask permission* to request their help in the future. But it does not stop here. Additionally, members of the virtual team are encouraged to maintain relationships with the customers.

I am only ten digits away.

One of my favorite sayings is that "I am only ten digits away." I actually prefer a phone call to email and can usually solve issues in a minute or two. Remember that a customer is also always only ten digits away when you desire to continue the relationship. Every day and every interaction brings a new opportunity to sell.

SALES PROFESSIONAL STORY

My sales professional friend, Ralph, was an expert in connecting with people and recognizing their needs. On one occasion I remember Ralph organizing a meeting between a customer and a team member from his company. The customer had a commitment to *his* customer and was not able to deliver because of an obstacle with his own internal processes. It seemed that their supplier had not delivered a critical element used in the production process. Ralph's company used a different vendor, but bought supplies in this same realm. Ralph's virtual team member arranged with his vendor to obtain the needed element for the customer. Everyone was delighted with the outcome.

Ralph's customer had become part of his virtual team, and Ralph knew how to tend to the needs of all his virtual team members. This scenario is an example of how Ralph saw the business value in helping his customer with an external problem. That customer is still buying from Ralph 20 years later.

Leaders and Builders of Virtual Teams

A virtual team builder or leader can be anyone. All professionals can leverage virtual teams for best success. It is natural for sales professionals and their organizations to start virtual teams. But when other professionals see how these teams work and that the company supports them, anyone can create a team for a greater purpose. Being a virtual team member contributes to job security. When members see the connection from their function to the customer, they can show how they contribute to the customer's satisfaction.

SALES PROFESSIONAL STORY

My dad, the ultimate sales professional that he was, created his virtual team through a logical, but intuitive, sense of customer needs. Those customers who were looking forward to their wedding day were only one set of customers. My dad had to rely on many others to ensure that he could create wedding pictures that would help the happy couple and their families delight in their memory of the wonderful day.

Creating a sales culture is for everyone.

Dad worked with people such as the film developer, the film supplier, the caterers, the florists, the facilities manager, his equipment provider, the couple's parents, and many others who happened onto the path between him and the couple. They all felt his intent and good wishes to make the pictures the best that they could be. My dad was creating value by leveraging his virtual team for the benefit of his clients. He understood that for his pictures to be excellent, everyone had to be connected.

The point is that you do not need to be part of a big company, or any company, to create a sales culture and a virtual team. My dad was a "one man band" who built his virtual sales culture by engaging and motivating the people who interacted with his clients, the brides and grooms. Virtual teams are for everyone.

Because Dad was so connected with all the members of his virtual team, including his clients, he received *lots* of referrals. His business grew thanks to the loyalty and confidence of his virtual team.

In Conclusion

The concept of a sales culture is only as valuable as the people involved. The success of the sales culture depends on the skills of the members, the abilities of a sales professional, and the support of the company to align them. All of these elements must be present and come together in a way that they complement each other. There is no one formula for success. Success always depends on the virtual team leader's ability to listen to each person, understand his or her needs, and then make a connection to the party who can most effectively meet those needs.

It is really fairly simple. Karen, Ralph, David, Jim, and my dad all created their sales culture intuitively for their organizations and their customers. That ability made them invaluable and their success was not hard to understand.

The concept of building a sales culture is a gift I have been given. Now, I want to give it to you so your selling is more successful and you make more money! So, who is on *your* virtual team? Get to work.

———　*Questions for you to think about*　———

1. Do you know on whom you can depend to help you accomplish specific tasks that the customer needs done?

2. Have you built an extended virtual team including the people who might need to support your primary virtual team?

3. Did you make a mind map or flow chart depicting your sales process as suggested earlier in this chapter? Has it changed after you have read this chapter? How does your mind map look now?

4. Have you sometimes not asked people to help because you thought they would say "No"?

5. Now that you have read this chapter why are you still selling by yourself?

6. Who will you add to your virtual team now?

4

Sales Campaigns in a Sales Culture

You can't lead people farther than you have gone yourself.
—Gene Mauch

By now you have seen that I am a passionate believer that everybody has a role in the sales process. Now we need to take a look at managing specific sales campaigns. Sometimes people think of a sales campaign as an advertising technique. For our purposes, a sales campaign is each unique sales opportunity.

Every time you identify a sales opportunity you launch a new sales campaign. In fact every conversation you have with a client has the potential to become a sales campaign. As a sales professional, you begin and manage the sales campaign by leveraging your virtual team. But the real work of a sales campaign is done by the members of the virtual team, which includes anyone and everyone who can help a client decide to buy. This is the essence of a sales culture.

Your sales campaign must be transparent to the entire virtual sales team. That means that every member of the virtual team sees:

- ❏ The whole picture of the campaign
- ❏ How he or she contributes
- ❏ The role each other team member plays

The members need to see the sales campaign as *good business;* that is, good for the company and for the client.

A virtual team member will not be afraid to ask questions to clarify product, client, or campaign information. Members must also feel free to raise questions, objections, and alternate solutions when they bring their knowledge and expertise to the table.

---

*Sales campaigns must be transparent
across the organization.*

Customer relationship management (CRM) software is a valuable tool that helps make the sales campaign transparent across your organization. We will talk more about CRM software in Chapter 8.

For a sales campaign to succeed every team member has to understand what it means to serve the client's needs. They all bring their collective talents to the table to support the ultimate customer solution. Hence, a deal closes and revenue comes with that close.

Regardless of the role a person plays within the organization, such as human resources, marketing, sales, research, or in another area; his or her work, directly or indirectly, systematically or otherwise, affects a customer's decision to buy.

Activating the Sales Campaign

There are several considerations involved in activating the sales campaign to make best use of the talents of all members of the organization.

❏ The sales professional builds the client relationship, interacting with the client to understand and establish agreement on the client's needs.

❏ The sales professional identifies everyone who can and should work on the virtual team to ensure the success of the sales campaign and the client's satisfaction.

❏ Team members identify other possible team members.

❏ Everyone on the team has the opportunity to build a relationship with the client.

The sales culture of the organization is enhanced and empowered by sales teams and their internal partners working together to bring the right people, products, and services to the market in the first place. The sales team and their colleagues build a client-centric mindset into an organization, using the sales culture environment as the catalyst.

SALES PROFESSIONAL STORY

Let me introduce sales professional Mike. Mike was a business development professional with a growing local bank. Mike's job was to get out and visit the local merchants near his branch and develop a relationship. His goal, of course, was to win their banking business. There was not a single prospect Mike met who had exactly the same requirements as another prospect. Not one! So every sales campaign had to be custom-tailored for that particular client.

It is no secret that banking is not the most flexible industry in the world. Mike knew that to win the business and satisfy the needs of the local merchants, he needed the input and support of several banking officials back at headquarters. That was no easy task in this era of banking regulations and rules. Mike had to first be a sales professional, wear his business hat, and make an honest evaluation as to whether the business the merchant wanted was *good* business for both the bank and the prospect.

When Mike decided that the business was worth pursuing he had to build his "case" to satisfy the customer. Then he presented that case to engage a virtual team of other banking professionals who would help him put the deal together. By making the sales campaign transparent, the virtual team also recognizes that the opportunity is good business. The teamwork created a "win-win" business deal.

Mike made sure that the conversations and communications were clear and always client-focused. He let everyone know that they were "in sales" not operating in a vacuum. Everyone zeroed in on the client. It's no surprise that Mike was a very successful and productive banker. People were always willing to be on his virtual team because Mike's deals made sense. Mike never let the team forget that the sales culture was all about the client.

VIRTUAL TEAM STORY

New equipment was introduced frequently at Xerox. Demo equipment would be installed at our customer visitor center, usually shortly before a formal launch. Technical personnel would install the new equipment and all sales professionals lined up to bring customers in to see a demonstration. New products were always exciting and, if we did our jobs right, we had prospects in the pipeline waiting to see the new machines.

There were always functional as well as technical issues that came up during the installation. Often the success of a sale depended on technicians helping sales professionals craft presentations based on the installation experiences of a technician. The technicians at Xerox had the most opportunities to learn about real world applications and the potential successes or failures of a product. Their experience was based on actual testing with clients as they used the equipment.

> *Often the success of a sale depended on technicians helping sales professionals.*

We all learned from the technicians how to show the new equipment at its best. The input and advice from the technicians allowed us to fine tune our demonstrations and our sales approach. The technicians were really connected to the client's needs, as they were the ones who worked with the client to maximize the equipment and its performance to best address that client's needs.

I remember a specific prospect I had all set up for the latest machine we were launching. I was so excited that the client showed faith in me and my company by agreeing to be the first to try the machine. I happily took the signed order back to the office. After showing the order to my manager, I went straight to the service department to start building my virtual sales team.

Whenever a new product is introduced, one of the technicians is assigned to be trained to assemble, install, and service the machine. I asked the sales manager which technician would be assigned to the new product I had just sold.

I then introduced myself to the technician, Phil, and began to tell him about the sale and the client's needs. That conversation made the sales campaign transparent to him. I invited him to join the virtual team. He was shocked that a sales rep took the time to engage him in the sales campaign.

The technician picked up on my building a relationship with the client. As a member of the virtual team on this transparent sales campaign, he was able to use his relational skills to be in constant contact directly with the client. Phil came in early the day of delivery and made sure he took extra time to assemble the new copier—his first!

You can imagine what happened next. The copier arrived and in the course of the installation, Phil encountered some problems and unexpected challenges. We learned some things about how to make that unit really run well. We talked throughout the day and we both kept the client informed.

Eventually that outstanding technician got the machine to run like a top! The client was very impressed and we won his loyalty for life. This is just a simple story, but it so well illustrates the nature of a sales culture. I became a friend of the service department and my clients were all taken care of.

---

*The client was very impressed and
we won his loyalty for life!*

Characteristics of a Virtual Team Member

Virtual team members can be identified by the following characteristics:

- ❏ Willingness to be part of the team
- ❏ Willingness to share their expertise for the benefit of the campaign
- ❏ Interest in seeing how their passion leads to a successful campaign

Sales professionals and virtual team members are very aware that they cannot sit in individual silos and expect long term success. The virtual team members are energized by working with clients and looking for opportunities to be a part of the sales process. For example, product development members understand that their work has to be done with the client in mind. They must seek out this context and take a risk when necessary. This is all done in the name of the customer.

Chapter 3 described the dynamics and fluidity that come with the phases of the sales campaign. Virtual teams will also sometimes change due to the product or service you sell or who your prospect is. Every virtual team exists to serve the specific sales campaign. Each sales opportunity becomes a distinct campaign supported by a distinct team.

Communicate Obsessively to Support the Sales Campaign

When I teach companies to build and manage their sales cultures, I always tell people they need to "communicate obsessively." Sometimes I get a puzzled stare but the concept is really simple. Sales professionals must communicate obsessively with their clients, partners, peers, management, and anyone who is part of their virtual team. Obsessive should not be confused with unnecessary; make every conversation or email count.

Obsessive communication also means that sales professionals and managers must make sure that the correct people around them are well-informed and feel as though they are part of the overall strategy. Communicating correctly and communicating often ensures that the people who can help close the deal are part of the big picture.

I have *always* felt motivated to do much more and do better when I *know what is going on* and what the goals are. Who can do their best when they are in the dark? What client wants to say "yes" when they don't have the facts and perhaps feel as though there is more they need to know?

Here are some important points to remember about communicating obsessively:

❑ Make communication direct, succinct, and related to the overall goal. Try not to get off the track or be tangential in your communication.

❑ Communicate when there is something to share or just to give a status check. Don't flood people with endless emails or conference calls.

❑ Whenever possible, let people hear your voice, your passion, and your conviction!

❑ Never *ever* miss a chance to tell people something important or critical.

❑ Never *ever* miss a chance to congratulate and thank virtual team members for their contributions.

Connecting Bottom Line Results to Virtual Team Characteristics

As the sales professional engages and builds the virtual team, a connection to the bottom line emerges. It is important that all members can relate to the overarching purpose, objective, and desired results of each sales campaign. Any time a virtual team is completely focused on serving the customer's needs, the bottom line improves.

Communication of critical information about customer needs on a regular basis is the job of the sales professional. Those who are serving the customer need to know how they affect the bottom line. Think of the receptionist in your office facility. That person has the important job of making the first impression on the client. Greeting the client in a way that demonstrates an understanding of what your company is all about is extremely important. When well-trained and knowledgeable about the client, your receptionist can set the tone for future interactions and experiences for the client. Your receptionist can be your best sales person.

Another example of successful virtual team interaction involves a member of the legal department. A particular client during the course of negotiations needs specific non-standard terms and conditions for the deal to close. The legal department representative can insist on meeting *only* the company standards for these terms or he or she can think like the client, understanding the client's needs. The legal department can arrange to meet those needs by allowing different terms and conditions to be used in the contract. The deal closes because the legal representative is a good virtual team member.

The bottom line is that people will respond positively to your request to be part of the virtual team if you are doing your job as a sales professional and creating a solid opportunity. Just ask!

SALES PROFESSIONAL STORY

Remember Ralph who put his client in touch with a new vendor? He was putting together a make or break deal for his sales year. This deal involved a very large conglomerate, and there were many points to be negotiated and worked out. One of the most nettlesome was a set of very specific terms and conditions that the client demanded as a pre-requisite to doing business. Those terms were not at all good for Ralph's company. When he found it impossible to reach a workable compromise he went to Jeff, the general counsel, and explained the client's dilemma.

Jeff offered a series of solutions that made sense. Jeff and Ralph collaborated on a series of options until they created a workable solution for the client.

Knowing he would not be as effective as general counsel in explaining the solution, Ralph asked Jeff to attend the next sales call. The client was impressed that the general counsel made the time for a direct meeting. Ralph's virtual team was so effective that they not only resolved the issues, but the deal size increased.

The client was impressed that the general counsel made the time for a direct meeting.

The point is that Ralph knew his limitations, internally found the right virtual team member to present a "win-win" solution, and actually closed the deal. The general counsel later commented that he was rarely asked to take part in the actual sales, and he now had a new appreciation for what sales professionals do. He found it very satisfying to be a virtual team member. That incident firmly instilled the attitude of being a part of a sales culture in Ralph's company.

This type of interaction at the level Ralph and Jeff accomplished it strongly contributes to the transparency of the sales campaign.

Organizational Behavior of the
Virtual Team in a Sales Campaign

Organizational behaviors like those of Ralph and Jeff demonstrate the value of virtual team members and contribute to the transparency of the campaign. Effective behavior is characterized by a rational approach to the campaign. The virtual team members come together with their egos in low gear. Everyone is willing to accept coaching from other team members.

A great example of this kind of reciprocal coaching on a virtual team is the story we looked at with Phil, the Xerox technician who eagerly received coaching on establishing a relationship with the client. In return, Phil coached me on technical features of the new product, and coached the client on maximizing the benefits of the new machine.

As a sales professional, you can take the lead by fearlessly engaging team members and encouraging them to speak up and share what they can contribute to the campaign. In your role you need to exhibit the skills of a quarterback, a manager, and a choreographer.

Client as Virtual Team Member

Another way to demonstrate value to your clients during a sales campaign is to provide education for them. This is a best practice, as well as mandatory, for a sales professional.

Organizations that stand for educating, advancing skills, and the art and science of sales will do better. Education leads to continuously improving performance and capacity of the sales organization. These practices allow virtual team members to share new learning with clients, which increases the company's credibility both with clients and internally. Sharing new learning leads to collaboration and generation of new concepts.

Becoming known as the thought leader in your industry and market is a significant differentiator and the hallmark of a great sales professional. Everyone in the organization is engaged in continuous learning and you make use of the shared thoughts from everyone in your organization.

Becoming known as the thought leader in your industry and market is a significant differentiator.

The companies that I have worked with, training them in sales culture principles, have invested money and time in the development and subsequent coaching of great sales professionals. The companies that make this investment, and do it with fervor, will create successful sales organizations that are the envy of their competitors!

It is important to think of clients, suppliers to you or to your clients, industry experts, potential clients, and any others who touch your sales campaign in any way as part of your virtual team.

Anyone who has an interest in your success is a part of your virtual team.

SALES PROFESSIONAL STORY

My dad is a perfect example of the concept of including clients, external suppliers, and many others on his virtual team. Dad was very dependent on others doing their jobs and doing them well. As a wedding photographer he needed his film suppliers, the labs that developed his pictures, the local florists and caterers, and so on to be focused on pleasing his clients.

In many ways, their products reflected my dad's quality of service to his clients. Dad needed to continuously tend to these members of his virtual team. Inspiring and leading others to work on your virtual team is a benefit to the team member, as well. Dad did this as a routine part of his daily work and recommended his virtual team members to clients, building credibility for them and their businesses. Clearly, his virtual team was not limited to his organization of one. He made good and efficient use of his team. Everyone thrived and profited in this environment my dad created.

Sales cultures only thrive when sales campaigns are transparent

In Conclusion

When all the members of the virtual team have a clear vision of the roles they play and vital contributions they make, the client becomes more invested in the process.

Educating the members of your internal virtual team, as well as your clients, is essential to building a strong virtual team. Everyone will make his or her best contribution if they thoroughly understand the workflow of the virtual team activities and have an appreciation for each person's role.

Questions for you to think about

1. Are all virtual team members part of your sales organization?

2. How might you invite people from outside your organization to become part of your virtual team?

3. When was the last time you invited your CFO or the general counsel to go on a sales call with you?

4. Have you ever invited a product developer or technician to meet the clients you work with?

Questions to share with internal members of your virtual team

1. Do you know who you supply with services and/or products?

2. Do you know who supplies you with services and/or products?

3. How do the tasks of your daily routine contribute to the close of a sales campaign?

4. Can you articulate your company brand, as it is perceived externally and as you convey it from the inside?

5

Creating a Sales Culture: Expectations and Accountability

You have to perform at a consistently higher level than others. That's the mark of a true professional.

—Joe Paterno

Are you expecting the right things? If you are building a sales culture, then your colleagues must be shaped by the expectation that they are part of a sales culture and accountable to the client and to one another. This means that sales leadership must create the expectation that the sales professionals will engage, motivate, and inspire others in the organization to be part of sales campaigns as we described in Chapter 4.

Sales professionals are accountable for providing direction to virtual team members on how to contribute effectively to the successful close of each sale. Other leaders in the organization also must create the environment that encourages participation and contribution of needed expertise. These leaders include the CEO, as well as the other executive managers.

A successful sales culture clearly lives and breathes on the expectation and accountability for virtual team members' behaviors. It is critical that members demonstrate behaviors that support the campaign and ultimately serve the client.

People deliver that which is expected.

A sales professional who demonstrates effective behaviors with clients can, in turn, set the expectation that the virtual team will adopt those behaviors.

Thinking in terms of a behavior as an expectation may be a new concept for a sales professional. Often expectations in a sales career are expressed in terms of numbers. Sales professionals are often rewarded for selling a certain number of units or adding a dollar amount to the company's bottom line.

Colleagues in other roles may not have had number-related goals and may be more accustomed to being evaluated on behaviors. What behaviors might be expected of a non-sales colleague? A marketing specialist could be expected to attend a sales call and begin to establish a relationship with the client. An HR specialist may be asked to keep sales culture expectations in mind when hiring new staff. A technician might be empowered to build a direct relationship with a customer. An R&D specialist might build the company's reputation by speaking at meetings with counterparts from other companies. All these actions respond to the expectations and accountability of the sales culture and also enhance each professional's RPi—Win-Win!

Communicating

Sales professionals are responsible and accountable for accurately relaying clients' needs and how each virtual team member can play a specific role to meet those needs. I have said many times that the sales professional is responsible to "communicate obsessively." This is critical to making sure that everyone has goals, outcomes, and the client objectives on the top of their minds.

Communicating obsessively sets the expectations for outcomes for the client, for virtual team members, and for the company. All virtual team members need to understand the benefits to the company when they meet or exceed the client's needs. Virtual team members are more motivated to participate in the sales campaign when they see the results of their contributions.

Virtual team members understand that there are benefits to all when they meet the client's needs.

Sales professionals reward the team members' contributions by publicly recognizing how the team members helped to close the sale. This recognition is very compelling to other virtual team members and attracts more colleagues in the company to join virtual teams.

Think about this: Why would people *not* want to be involved where revenue and profits are concerned? Have you ever heard of anyone losing out when they are known to help close business?

If virtual team members are not seeing results and being recognized for their contributions, you don't have a sales culture. You need to start applying what you are learning in this book. Regardless of the economy, being part of a revenue-generating team is always a good career strategy.

Acknowledgement and rewards help to create an environment that sustains success in future sales campaigns. When everyone is in sales and each is specifically recognized for his or her contribution, then everyone can feel the power and excitement of working on the virtual team toward a shared goal.

Whenever I get the chance to talk about this part of creating a sales culture, one of the first questions I get is how to respond when a prospective virtual team member asks "Why should I be involved? I don't get any commission like those sales guys."

Here is my answer:

> It is often thought that sales people make more money than everyone else. That is not always true. A sales professional's compensation is usually comparable with the compensation of other professionals.

> As employees, we each contribute our own expertise to the company. Every employee is then compensated for his or her expertise. We don't all receive the same paycheck but our compensation is based on the skills, education, and training we bring to the table. When we all contribute to winning sales campaigns, we increase the company's bottom line. Increasing the bottom line creates a healthy economical environment for all.

Communicating this understanding is critical to motivating effective collaboration among virtual team members.

Whenever I have seen the opportunity to meet a client's need through the development of a virtual team, I can say with certainty that building that team has been a fun and easy task. I have found that people want to be asked and in most circumstances they will say, "Yes."

> *To get people to be a part of your virtual*
> *team and share their expertise: Just ask!*

I remember a time when I was the recipient of a request to help with a deal. At the time I did not realize that I was being asked to share my knowledge and that this was a very great compliment. At the time I was in a sales role that was parallel to the core business. I was so thrilled that someone recognized my knowledge as something that they needed, I agreed to be a part of that virtual team. Working with the clients gave me valuable and robust insight into how the sales professional was building the solution.

This Is What a Sales Culture Looks Like

Recent experiences with Continental Airlines give me the impression that their employees are part of a vibrant sales culture. I experienced this not once but several times when I have flown with them.

The best example is the time I was stuck for seven hours in San Jose airport due to a mechanical problem with the aircraft. Continental had to fly in a mechanic and plane parts from Houston. The local staff was exceptional. They communicated with us regularly on what was happening, they served refreshments in the waiting area, and handled a long line of aggravated passengers who were missing connections. They made sure that anyone who missed a connection had hotel accommodations and they picked up the tab for the hotel.

In addition, a gate agent personally went out to the tarmac and retrieved my bag so I could get my work materials and spend the downtime getting some work done.

Every person I witnessed was a terrific sales professional that day. They worked together, were unflappable in the face of a totally uncontrollable situation, and did a fantastic job. Continental earned my loyalty that day. I should also note that a few weeks later I received an unsolicited letter and a discount coupon from Continental. The letter apologized for the delay that day and explained in detail what had occurred.

The bottom line on this experience is that every Continental employee I interacted with behaved as if they were accountable for my satisfaction. The airport crew, the gate agent, and the representative who wrote to me later all demonstrated their accountability.

SALES PROFESSIONAL STORY

Julia, the CEO of a financial services staffing firm with a growing sales culture, strives to help all employees to be customer-centric. Her behaviors are specifically intended to value the expertise of each team member and to reward involvement to support successful sales campaigns. Julia's behaviors include:

❑ Continuously communicating objectives and goals as they pertain to each client

❏ Continuously acknowledging individual contributions to those goals

❏ Expecting that all virtual team members are accountable to produce a successful sales campaign

These specific behaviors provide many informal examples of team contributions that will be rewarded and tell everyone in the organization that the virtual team members are appreciated. Julia never fails to connect goals to each person's accountability to achieve them. After all, if each sales professional in the company is accountable to meet and exceed quotas, and if we are all in sales, then are we all not accountable? Remember—No sales equals no company.

Julia was not unique. She just behaved as she expected others to behave. And this is the key to leadership in a sales culture environment. Commitment from the top executive sets the expectation that all other leaders, especially including the sales leaders, will be client-centric in their expectations of all organizational members.

SALES PROFESSIONAL STORY

Jonathan was a CEO who understood that he set the tone for the sales culture to flourish. Jonathan was a people person. He knew that all of the good ideas did not matter if the team did not resonate with the client. As a result, he helped to create a sales culture because he put himself front and center with the client and listened, responded, and acted deliberately. At the time we did not refer to this as a sales culture, but it was easy to see that he was championing a sales culture. He modeled obvious client-centric behavior and he showed that he valued everyone's input. We all wanted to work with Jonathan because he held himself accountable to the client and to us. He supported us to deliver quality to the client and led us in maintaining a strong sales culture.

Executives' Roles in Creating Sales Culture Environment

Defining what a sales culture is and what it looks like is important to setting an environment of accountability. The most important aspect of this accountability is for the executives to hold themselves accountable to this culture. The executives must be aware of the implications of their behaviors as they motivate, inspire, and reward the contributions of virtual team members. As leaders, executives must be willing to share observations and coach one another on behaviors that create the sales culture. If they cannot help each other, then they probably will not be able to help the members of their organization.

Executives must hold themselves accountable to the sales culture.

The virtual team concept should begin with the virtual team of executives.

Let me talk for a moment more about Jonathan. I mentioned that he held us all accountable to deliver, to engage each other, and finally to create a solution that would delight our client. The best part about Jonathan as a CEO is that he did not hold himself above the fray. He made sure he communicated and did the right thing. He made sure we knew and saw that he was engaged and he communicated to us his deliverables and responsibilities. He was an outstanding CEO to create a sales culture because he knew he was ultimately responsible for the company and we needed the clients to see our vision and engage us.

Sales Culture Sustains Sales Skills

A sales culture thrives because sales skills are maintained with a commitment at the top of the organization. Executive decision-makers must continue to support the sales culture. To guarantee long-term success, the clients of this culture are all of the people who can make a difference, including those who create and set strategic direction for the company. Without buy-in from all these stakeholders, the sales culture will not live.

The clients of this culture are all of the people who can make a difference, including those who create a strategic direction for the company

---

Another critical point here is that a sales culture creates an environment that encourages peer-to-peer coaching and accountability. Once sales cultures are understood and established, they only thrive when people hold each other accountable. The culture is initialized and grows throughout the organization as all leaders and individuals coach and reinforce each other's essential selling skills. Coaching happens everywhere; it may be planned or spontaneous.

A great sales professional sees a coaching opportunity and provides that training.

Peer-to-peer coaching starts with embracing the notion of what is right for your organization. When peer-to-peer coaching is a common practice, with no negative repercussions for peers to hold each other accountable, outcomes are positive. People begin to behave and talk differently; they begin to behave as part of the sales culture that is the new norm. But it does "take a village" to reinforce these new behaviors. Sales culture is not mandated, it is *created* through the right behaviors that are sustained at the top and rewarded throughout the organization.

Sales culture is not mandated, it is created through the right behaviors.

Clearly, talk alone can't force people to change. Reinforcement of new behaviors through coaching, training, workshops, and peer-to-peer interactions allows people to embrace and implement a sales culture environment.

When you hear something that does not seem to reflect the sales culture that you are intending to build, don't look at this as necessarily negative. It may just reflect a new need for clarification on how people might effectively work together.

An example of this type of conflict happened one day when I was monitoring the integrated work of two engineers who were part of my virtual team at Xerox. They were not aligned on the best way to solve a customer's problem. They were challenging each other and, at times, not listening. Something had to change or the project was going to fail.

After some mutual accountability and some gentle coaching, they started to consider the common goal, and not the individual value that each sought. They started to see each other's perspective and they started to work together, leaving their egos at the door. Their solution was a combination of their ideas and they seemed to come away from the incident with a greater respect for each other. This was a remarkable experience in that we could really feel like we were all part of the same virtual team. The motivator for all of us was ultimately the customer. We all felt this and contributed accordingly to please the customer.

SALES PROFESSIONAL STORY

Remember Karen who guided a Xerox sales campaign to win a national contract with a large utility? Here is another lesson in that story. Karen figured out the reason that we had originally been left out of the bidding. It seems the sales representative who had been in contact with that utility was a little weak on relational skills. Karen mentored that rep, coaching her on relational and communication skills. With Karen's support and encouragement the rep honed her skills, became a much stronger presence in the marketplace, and began to establish her RP. Sales cultures routinely provide this kind of growth opportunity for the individual.

The Ultimate Success Story

My dad's virtual team was ever-changing and very inclusive. It was continuously evolving, but all knew that they were members and what was expected of them. The satisfaction of the client was expected in no uncertain terms. And my dad established this understanding in subtle ways, by example. He never had to say that the client was the point of all endeavors. Everyone on his virtual team knew this to be the case because of the way he conducted his business. They worked and celebrated success together.

Dad was a great sales professional because he did not take his selling casually. He was focused and pro-active. Dad was a very outgoing, jovial person, but he was much deeper than that. He wasn't the guy who showed up with a box of donuts. What he did was show up *fully present!* One of his greatest qualities was his sincere concern for people.

He always knew and cared about what was going on in the lives of the people he interacted with. He remembered to ask about how a spouse or child was recovering from an illness or celebrating a victory. When someone told him about a problem or asked for his advice, which happened often, he was a caring listener and offered sound and thoughtful advice.

His ultimate success was articulated by many on his virtual team when they asked when his next wedding was going to be. They asked to help him. They all wanted to be a part of his virtual team, contributing as an expert in their part to fulfill the client's needs and expectations.

In Conclusion

Sales culture doesn't happen in a vacuum. Sales culture happens because people proactively demand the right behaviors. Sales culture happens because people hold each other accountable for behaviors that go beyond the metrics. In a sales culture, success depends on the combination of the right behaviors, accountability, and metrics.

Questions for you to think about

1. Do you know what is expected of you and how you will be held accountable?

2. Do the executives in your organization hold themselves accountable for what is expected of them?

3. When was the last time you asked for clarification on expectations?

4. Are the expectations for everyone on your virtual team clear to the whole team?

5. Does everyone on the virtual team know what the customer's expectations are?

6. Are you taking advantage of opportunities to provide coaching?

6

How Am I Doing?

Timid salesmen have skinny kids.

—Zig Ziglar

The ultimate client experience happens when your client is a partner to the sales cycle and in the innovation strategy of the company. When clients are integrated into research and planning, there is significant sustainability built into those processes. A sales culture supports these important relationships.

Clients are partners on your virtual team.

Ensuring a Satisfied Client

How do you know that a client is satisfied? As we have established, the client is the central member of your team. The sales professional takes the responsibility for focusing on the client and checking on his or her satisfaction.

As a sales professional, you are communicating obsessively with all virtual team members, including the clients. So, you will not be caught off guard hearing that a client is not satisfied.

Communicating is not just asking for the order, it is a continuous and obsessive process of checking in. The best sales professionals ask "How am I doing?" This is not easy to do, but those who do it are always better off. When you show the client that you sincerely care about their business, the relationship can't help but get better.

There are a couple of ways to evaluate how you are doing in satisfying a client. Ask the client routinely how you are doing in serving his needs. The best sales professional does this as part of the sales campaign, even asking for specifics of what is going well and what could be improved.

Asking for feedback this way can scare some sales reps but not sales professionals. There is no better way to gauge the health of your sales campaign and the effectiveness of your virtual team.

There is really no mystery as to how to know if a client is satisfied. You just ask.

I used to be terrified to ask anything that would invite an answer that might not be positive. But instinctively I knew that avoiding the question was not going to work for my career long term. The funny thing is that I often wanted to ask questions like "Are you happy?" or "How am I doing?" It gnawed away at me that I was so close to asking and I just never did. I felt like a wimp!

One day I was with my client, Frank. I really liked Frank and I knew he liked me, as well. That day he looked at me and said, "You know, Todd, you always ask me for the order; but you never ask how we are doing." That shocked me because I have always prided myself on taking a deep interest in my clients.

I must have had a totally dumbfounded look on my face. So he smiled and said "Todd, ask me . . . go ahead . . . it won't hurt." So, I said, "Frank, how am I doing as a sales rep?" and held my breath. Frank smiled and said, "I am glad you asked!"

Then we had an amazing two-hour conversation on why he did business with me and with my company. We covered so many areas that I lost track of time and had a great experience. From that day on, I began to ask my clients the hard questions about me and my company. And each time the same thing happened: The client and I became closer and developed a tighter professional relationship which led to more sales. Many of them became friends and mentors over the years. I will always be grateful to Frank, for helping me to grow as a sales professional. Learning to ask, "How am I doing?" helped me to establish better relationship portability throughout my career. This may be the greatest tool you can use to increase your RPi.

Using Metrics

Sales professionals are typically evaluated on the number of calls, meetings and proposals they track. In addition metrics may record the networking and speaking activities of the virtual team. If you also develop some metrics with a client to ensure that you agree on what determines customer satisfaction, you will never be surprised.

Continuous check-in on the metrics is an unbeatable practice and will lead to an increased success rate.

A client might say that things are going well, he or she is satisfied, and also suggest some ways to improve. When this happens, you know that this client is feeling comfortable as part of the virtual team. When a client shares a concern, he or she believes that improvement will occur. This kind of dialogue revolves around my concept of obsessive communication.

You have to measure your business. Sales culture goes beyond what is measured in a siloed business. The success of a sales culture is based on measuring behaviors and implementing accountability.

A sales professional should not be afraid to hear about concerns and things to improve. You do not always have to hear positives, and you won't! If the client is willing to tell you negatives and still be a client, then the relationship is solid. You can use the shared information to help you create a more satisfying product or service for your client. This is an indication that your sales culture and your virtual team are working. You client has trust and confidence that negatives can be turned into positives.

If the client is willing to tell you negatives and still be a client, then the relationship is solid.

A sales professional must have the confidence to ask for feedback, not just to avoid losing business, but more importantly, to improve the business and the client's satisfaction. Communicating about satisfaction is an opportunity for sales professionals to check in with all the members of the virtual team on a regular basis.

SALES PROFESSIONAL STORY

Sales professional Lenny was one of the most remarkable colleagues I have ever worked with. He checked in with his client so well and built such a rock solid relationship, that he was able to do something extremely rare. At the beginning of each fiscal year, all the sales professionals in the company received sales goals for the next 12 months. Lenny would then share that goal with his client and ask the client to agree to a sizable amount of that business! The client agreed to be part of Lenny's virtual team by buying based on behaviors and accountability. He knew he could depend on Lenny's sales culture and virtual team to take good care of him. This was a most outstanding example of mutual trust and confidence.

Sharing Client Knowledge with the Rest of the Virtual Team

Communicating obsessively happens in every format and medium—emails, conference calls, meeting people face-to-face. Regardless of your mode, communication should be continuous, whether planned or serendipitous.

When virtual team members realize that these conversations are important, action-oriented, and helpful, and never of a critical nature; they will participate positively as well. The virtual team members must see that the sales professional supports them and assumes that they will do the right thing regarding the client's satisfaction.

Inviting Your Client to be Part of Research and Planning

Clients hold a wealth of information on your next steps in developing your business. Other virtual team members can look to the client for leadership in creating effective solutions for future business innovations. Engaging clients this way builds security into your product development efforts.

Engaging clients in future innovations builds security into your product development.

When I was with a startup in the late 1990s, we were selling products and services that were very cutting edge—really cool concepts that bucked the trends. We needed clients to buy from us to prove the viability of the concept and the company so we could confidently raise money. This was more challenging than selling in the traditional way. We needed a small cadre of early adopters, who really understood and were excited about our value proposition, and were willing to be on the edge with us!

Early adopters like our client, Joe, became great clients and advocates for us. We involved these clients as early as possible in the design and creation of their solution. Joe was introduced and encouraged to interact with the entire virtual team. We all knew Joe and had a very good understanding of his requirements, which were constantly changing, but changing with the entire virtual team playing a role. It was a partnership of sales culture at its finest.

Motivating the Client to Participate in Your Business Development Efforts

How will you motivate clients to participate? Why would the client *not* want to participate? If your client is disinterested, too busy, or too disconnected to participate, then your conversation has taken the wrong direction and you have some work to do. If the sales professional has asked the wrong questions, it can seem that the sales professional is asking the client to do his job or provide service to his company.

Ongoing conversations including the client, the sales professional, and the virtual team should show the client the high esteem in which you hold him or her. You are really expressing confidence and value in that client.

When a client entrusts their solution and, perhaps, business well-being, to you, it is not hard for them to want to be involved in the process. The engagement does not have to be structured and formal. You can engage them in a way that is professional and thoughtful about the way they work and their desire to be involved. Be sure to use their language and their cultural comfort level to be as informal or formal as the client needs in your interactions.

SALES PROFESSIONAL STORY

As a sales professional with a "dot com" company that developed e-learning products, I encouraged my entire virtual team to interact, check, and double-check with our client from day 1. We were developing a brand new e-learning program for our client, so we checked frequently throughout the development process to confirm the validity of the program.

I reminded the virtual team to keep egos in neutral (or leave them at the door) and keep the client at the center of the virtual team.

Along the way we made numerous adjustments to our product. In the end we arrived at an e-learning program that our customer was more than happy to accept. As a team we saw the ultimate sales campaign success.

Infusing Innovation into Your Sales Culture

When sales professionals and all other virtual team members think of being creative and innovative as a daily practice, new business opportunities arise. A creative mindset enables virtual teams to think of new and ingenious ways to use current resources or to create new resources and opportunities in response to challenges.

Innovating means that you are open to opportunities. In a sales culture, people are free to connect and engage in opportunistic conversations. The environment should encourage these connecting and creative conversations. In a sales culture, sales professionals encourage research and development colleagues to communicate with clients and to recognize potential opportunities. Together clients and R&D could feasibly initiate the next sales campaign.

Next steps in implementing new ideas become part of the strategy team's responsibility. Setting the expectation that people should converse creatively is critical to business development. A sales culture environment encourages this kind of creative conversation. And the sales professional is right in the middle, leading the charge to do the right thing, and to challenge the company, the virtual team, and the client.

In our e-learning program development, for example, we learned valuable information by frequently checking in with the client. We were able to alter and enhance our product based on the client's input. The result was a product we knew would meet, or preferably, exceed the client's requirements.

SALES PROFESSIONAL STORY

Once again my dad is a wonderful example of a sales professional. Dad was never afraid to check in with his customers or any member of his virtual team. He checked in all day with his brides and grooms. In addition he never missed a chance to check in with the musicians, wait staff, or venue managers. He always wanted to know what they saw and heard.

He also never missed a chance to thank someone on his virtual team for contributing to his success. I remember, in particular, a time when something on Dad's camera was broken. His camera vendor went out of his way to repair Dad's camera in record time, so he arrived at the wedding on time. Dad was lavish in his gratitude to his vendor and further cemented his loyalty.

Dad communicated constantly and, yes, obsessively with the brides, the grooms, and his whole virtual team with the result of many, many spectacular wedding days.

In Conclusion

The best result of having a sales culture is that the internal and external clients are all satisfied. Getting good feedback from external clients and employees is the best of all worlds for the one in charge. This has to lead to satisfaction for the leader who will experience a solid and sustainable level of success.

Recognizing the value of the sales culture, seeing deals close, generating new revenue, increasing internal satisfaction of workers . . . these are all the makings of a thriving environment, a sales culture.

Questions for you to think about

1. Is your client willing, perhaps eager, to brainstorm with you about new business services or products you might develop?

2. Does the client feel valued?

3. When was the last time you asked a client "How Am I Doing?"

4. If your answer is, "It's been a while." Stop reading, pick up the phone, and check in with your favorite client. *Now!*

5. If you are checking in with your client, does your relationship tend to become better or worse?

6. Does your client take your phone calls?

7. Is your client making you a priority?

8. Are you a preferred vendor or just another sales rep?

9. Where does your client fit on the RP grid?

7

Sales Culture Rides the Trends and Bests the Competition

Never compete alone.

—Todd Cohen

In this chapter we will explore creating and demonstrating your value to prospects and clients. We will look at current trends and competition, and how a sales culture positions you to leverage them for new and sustainable value.

Real Value for Today

Real value in any economy depends on creating great professional relationships through networking. There is tremendous value in the collective wisdom and capability of the right virtual team performing for the client.

Another huge value is created by differentiating between:

- ❏ Sales skills and sales culture—Sales skills are a subset of competencies of a sales culture.
- ❏ Sales training and sales culture—Sales training is one of the requirements to sustaining a sales culture.
- ❏ Sales metrics and sales performance—Sales metrics are just one way of determining sales performance.

Understanding these concepts puts you in a position to leverage the complexity of the current sales climate.

Sales cultures leverage the
world and its complexity.

Sales Culture Uncovers and Creates Real Value

Yes, sales culture does uncover real value exponentially, because it leverages the value of everybody in the company. Selling happens because of what each individual does. Not everyone calls on prospects or hands out brochures, but everyone does represent the company in whatever they do. Everyone knows that you do not have a viable company if you cannot sell what you make.

When someone from research and development presents at a conference of his or her peers, that presentation represents the quality of your company. This is an example of how anyone can start a sales campaign.

Value Proposition in the Sales Culture

Everybody has to understand the company's common value proposition. The value proposition of your company is a statement of the benefits and value you deliver to your clients. Everyone needs to understand how your value is perceived by the clients, how to position it, and how to support the sales team as they sell it. When everyone understands these concepts, they can form and leverage the professional relationships of a sales culture. They are all contributing to the sales culture and to the value of the company.

When a sales culture is operating efficiently, everyone is working to support sales. They all understand how they contribute their subject-matter expertise to sustain the company's value proposition. Because of the diversity of skills and expertise, they are not just thinking sales, they are thinking about the client, quality, and future needs as they do their work. They feel a sense of responsibility and accountability to consider clients and their needs every day.

Some of the dot com companies that popped up in the 1990s offered a product or service based on one person's perception of a value proposition. Some entrepreneurs charged ahead with a new business without external validation. They didn't build a sales culture with input from employees or prospects. They didn't establish a value proposition that employees could support. It's no surprise that those are among the dot coms that crashed and burned.

The real values you create in your sales culture can help your company to accelerate growth and results in the current environment including the following:

❏ Competitive forces
❏ Globalization and technologies
❏ Sustaining value proposition

Sales Culture Identifies and Manages Competitive Forces

If everyone is engaged in the selling process, everyone brings a unique perspective about what the competition is doing. The competition is better viewed collectively than individually. Everyone can engage in the business case to analyze and understand the competition. Analyzing the competition also promotes an understanding of where you stand and how your value proposition is being accepted and/or leveraged by your competition.

The competition is better viewed collectively than individually.

When your competition is moving in a curious direction, isn't it time for you to determine why? This analysis may give you insights into your client's future needs—or even needs that are peripheral to your value proposition—that you might consider satisfying. New products come about through this process. Don't overlook the opportunity to consider all possibilities. With all of your organizational members thinking competitively, your company is much better able to manage its competitive forces.

In all cases, your virtual team must know where you stand and what your value proposition is. Competition is a critical part of the selling process. Knowing your competition is most vital to creating successful sales campaigns. The virtual team will leverage this knowledge in every task in a sales campaign.

Sales Cultures Are Global

Sales cultures are hemisphere-independent. With internet connectivity and global accessibility to information, why would your virtual team be limited to your zip code? Virtual teams are exponentially powered by technology including social networking tools and web-based networking groups.

When technology is combined with the physical mobility of your employees, your company can have a global presence with very little extra effort. Members of your virtual team can do business around the globe from anywhere they happen to be.

In a sales culture, the members of your virtual team are empowered to see that your company never misses an opportunity. All team members can add new members to the team. All team members can recommend new business possibilities with new prospects. You may soon find yourself learning to say, "We are all in sales," in different languages.

Sales Culture Sustains the Value Proposition You Have Created

The value you have created is not just product value or company value. The real value of the sales culture is the client and internal relationships of the virtual team. This team is assembled to be client-focused. Their job is to maintain a client focus that maintains sales. The culture sustains the motivation throughout the organization and keeps everyone focused on contributing to the value proposition. The virtual team is where the sales culture comes alive.

*The real value of the sales culture is the client
and internal relationships of the virtual team.*

SALES PROFESSIONAL STORY

My dad's value proposition went far beyond just taking pictures. In his quest to make the bridal couple's day perfect he kept in close communication with all the other members of the virtual team at the wedding. Knowing what was happening with the parents, caterer, florist, and musician, he never missed the important photos of family members, cake-cutting, center pieces, or first dances.

Can a Sales Culture Mitigate Competitive Forces?

Competition can not only be mitigated, but also leveraged, by a sales culture. If you can manage your knowledge of the competition, then you can also manage the competition. A sales culture allows you to manage, mitigate, and leverage your competition.

Managing competitiveness can be a complex process in your sales culture and could lead to a potential risk. The risk lies in the overzealousness of a virtual team member who might misrepresent what your company can do or the value that you can provide to your clients.

At the other end of that spectrum, you will have some people who will resist the opportunity to participate. Perhaps they just want to be left alone to do their jobs. Their contributions, then, are a loss to the sales culture of the company, as they are not out in the mainstream saying good things or collecting valuable information.

In my experience as a vice president of sales for a large company, I was responsible for the integration of several lines of the business. The head of each line had his own agenda and objective. The only way to create a sales culture was to convince them to focus on what was good for the client not for their agenda.

A balance of independence and interdependence of virtual team members can be difficult for leaders to enforce. A good sales professional can often encourage the reluctant colleague to participate by showing him or her the importance of the role he or she plays in the sales campaign. Other colleagues cannot be drawn into a sales culture until senior leadership decides to declare participation mandatory.

Sales Culture Retains Value Regardless of Trends

Sales culture is not temporary. You need it to continue to sustain all your value in changing trends. The basic premise of sales culture is that it increases the chance that your sales campaign will succeed. Your drive for more business goes beyond an individual example of innovating. More than that, ongoing adoption of this client-centric process plays a never ending role in keeping companies and their members from retreating back to their silos.

In Conclusion

Sales reps in a siloed culture let competition frustrate them because they see their competitors as someone they have to defeat alone.

This task seems huge and unwieldy. Sales professionals—regardless of their titles—from across functional areas can successfully defeat the competition by leveraging the collective knowledge of the virtual team. Don't compete alone.

Questions for you to think about

1. Do you know your competition's value proposition?

2. Does your virtual team know your competition's value proposition?

3. Do you and your virtual team know your client's value proposition?

4. Do you think your competition knows your value proposition?

5. How are you leveraging technology to build your sales culture and your virtual team?

6. Why are you competing alone?

8

A Framework for a Sales Culture: How to Build Yours

A sale is not something you pursue: it's what happens
when you are immersed in serving your customer.

—Unknown

You are probably wondering, "What do I do now? Where do I start? What are the steps to create and nurture a sales culture?"

Sales culture is a combination of
attitudes, behaviors, and tools.

Here is your framework for establishing and growing your own robust sales culture. The following figure shows the cyclical nature of the sales culture. Communication throughout the whole virtual team includes the public support of the sales culture by senior management, sales leadership, sales professionals, everyone in the company, and all clients and prospects.

Decide right now before you read any further what you want for your sales organization. Do you want to do things that commit you to a road of success or are you "ok" with mediocrity? Sure, it's a rhetorical question, but only you can make this decision for your company and your career.

"We Are All in Sales"

This one is simple. Start using the statement, "We are all in sales," in your day-to-day interactions and as part of your sales vocabulary. Once you start using the words, you will start acting them and executing on them. These words remind people that everything they do has an impact on prospects and clients. If people nod in agreement and then go back to work in their silos, you have a choice. If you choose to hold your colleagues accountable, the sales culture will grow. If you don't, silos will flourish. Regardless of whether you are a CEO, a sales leader, an individual contributor, or whatever your role, the sales culture thrives by holding each other accountable to be "in sales." What you do delivers value to every sale.

Here is a key point that everyone should remember. Being in a sales culture does *not* mean stopping the job you were hired to do and "doing" sales. It means that in a sales culture everything we do *is sales* and has a sales component to it. Everything you do generates revenue either directly or indirectly.

Being in a sales culture does not mean stopping the job you are paid to do and "doing" sales. Everything we do is sales.

Demonstrate Executive Level Buy-In

The first step to establishing a sales culture is to get the buy-in of the executive level management in your company. The CEO should also be the CSO (Chief Sales Officer). Once the senior managers very publicly acknowledge the need for a sales culture, you are on your way. This commitment to harnessing the sales efforts of the entire company goes beyond the sales team. In order to establish the sales culture, the mantra must be, "Everyone is in sales." Lip service does not count and it does not pay the bills or the salaries.

After a presentation on sales culture for 75 senior leaders in a company, the CEO stood up and asked this question, "Todd, what can I do as CEO to start to build a sales culture?" Just asking that question in front of 75 senior leaders made a dramatic statement.

My answer then is exactly what I am telling you now. "A sales culture is based on the *behaviors* of all the employees. As CEO you are in the position to hold senior leadership accountable for their behavior."

Businesses fall into one of two categories—those that are mediocre and those that are doing well. A common fault of mediocre companies is that management presses the sales team to sell more without holding the rest of the company accountable for their behavior. A company that is doing well is more likely to have a sales culture where everyone is held accountable and everyone has a line of sight to revenue.

If you are the senior manager or the CEO, you can make the decision to set your organization on a path that screams success and not mediocrity! Take a breath and just make the commitment. If you are a sales leader, your job is to convince the senior leadership to make that decision. Build your case on facts and not emotion, but don't forget the passion of the sales culture environment we have talked about in the last seven chapters.

A CRM Can Enhance Sales Campaign Transparency

As a sales leader, and especially as the senior leader of the organization, you must make sure that all sales campaigns are transparent to the whole virtual team. Transparency comes from the words you use, and it starts when you encourage, inspire, and motivate the members of your virtual team. Transparency results from holding your team accountable for behaviors.

The key to success in a sales culture is to make it easy for people to see how their contribution affects sales. A customer relationship management (CRM) software program is an excellent tool for a transparent sales campaign, but you can have transparency without one. My dad had transparency before CRMs were invented.

If you choose to use a CRM, keep the following guidelines in mind:

❑ The CRM you choose acts as a lens into the sales campaign pipeline for the entire virtual team. Without a tool to facilitate a common view, people will be tempted to retreat to their silos and your sales culture can wither and die.

❑ The key to successfully using the CRM is to make it a living and breathing repository for the sales culture and not a just a warehouse for data input. In a sales culture, we all hold each other accountable. In the use of the CRM it is usually effective for sales leadership to see that the whole sales team is using the CRM. In turn, senior leadership then holds sales leadership accountable.

❑ Once every conversation in the sales culture is based on the facts in the CRM, you have achieved a transparency that will be the envy of your competitors. Then every interaction, every email, every conversation, every connection is about the value proposition.

❑ Once you have a common conversation you now can develop robust sales processes that fire up the sales culture. Your territory and account reviews as well as weekly plans and reviews all are based on the input and output from the CRM.

Selling is not a spectator sport. No one can sit in a silo and watch. Everyone needs to know how to use the CRM. As with any new system implemented in any organization, there will be a certain amount of resistance to using it and there will be a learning curve involved.

The first step to make the use of a CRM as easy as possible for people to learn, is to make the CRM accessible to anyone on the virtual team who contributes their expertise to the sales process. The CRM then becomes the focal point for consistency when employees talk about the sales culture. As new people are hired at your company, make CRM training part of the routine new employee orientation training.

Once everyone is on board with the CRM, it is not just a repository of facts, the CRM tells the narrative of the sales culture, its knowledge, and its learning.

Create a Non-Siloed Sales Team

The next step in the evolution of your sales culture is to make sure that your sales team is not encased in a silo. After senior management gives the sales culture their blessing, the sales team becomes the first place from which the sales culture springs forth. The sales team knows by now that they can't set themselves apart and try to do it all alone. Creating a silo-free environment starts with hiring and training sales professionals who "get" this. Once the sales team is out of their silo, they lead the way for the other teams to break down their own walls.

❏ Recruiting the right sales professionals starts by working with your HR departments and the other leadership areas to develop the profile of the right candidate to fit in a sales culture.

❏ When you collaborate with the HR group, you are living the sales culture principle. Help HR help you find and develop sales professionals who have the right set of skills that foster a sales culture.

Operate with Virtual Teams

We have talked a great deal about the practicality of the virtual team. The sales culture depends on the concept and execution of seamless virtual teams to thrive and to rocket the business forward. The virtual team concept should not be negotiable, and it costs nothing to create.

The virtual team does require a commitment to understanding the concept of a virtual team and acting accordingly. The sales team needs to know they are free and empowered to engage resources and invite people to be on the virtual team. It's up to the senior leadership and the sales leadership to make being a part of the virtual team expected and not optional.

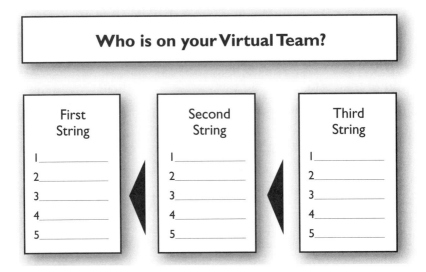

Who Is on Your Virtual Team?

In the illustration above you can see that your virtual team is made up of three strings. Your first string team members are the people that you connect with on a daily or weekly basis. When they are out in the workplace, they are passionate and engaged about what you offer. They are thinking and talking about what you can do for the client.

Your second string are people you connect with on a monthly or bi-monthly basis. They are also engaged in what you offer and what you do for the client, but are not as close to you or as involved as the first string. The third string are people you interact with occasionally.

As you continually grow as a sales professional and reevaluate your relationships, look for ways that you can move your second string team members to first string. Try to engage your third string members to the point that they become second string. In this way, you strengthen your virtual team and increase your RPi.

Train Everyone in Sales Principles

Sales culture means everyone is in sales—so why would you *not* train the entire company in the basics of sales? This is a bold and courageous step. In my work delivering this kind of training with my sales culture workshops, I have seen some amazing results and new energy. The conversation about sales culture transparency takes on a new life. People *want* to help and be a part of the revenue-producing groups. If there is to be a sales culture, then everyone needs a basic level of sales knowledge.

A shared sales vocabulary leads to results that everyone understands.

What is really impressive is that most people have some basic sales *instincts* and this translates well into an understanding of sales. Here is the most important point about sales training: When you train *horizontally and vertically,* you create a sales culture that cannot be stopped.

If sales training is only available to the sales team, that indicates there is a silo. Sales training for the whole organization defines and creates a sales culture. It extends the value of the sales training and differentiates you from your competition.

Sales training for the whole organization defines and creates a sales culture.

Asking for the Sale

Here is an example of an important aspect of a sale that everyone should know. It is very basic that everyone should learn when and how to ask for the order. Some very proficient business and sales people never get to the point of asking for the order. Are they being too polite, or are they afraid of hearing "No"? The client is waiting for you to ask for the sale. He is not going to interrupt you to ask to buy! You have to have an awareness and ability to ask for the order whenever the moment seems right. That right moment is usually when you feel that you have earned the right to ask.

The client is waiting for you to ask for the sale.
He is not going to interrupt you to ask to buy!

I was on the buying side of a sales call one afternoon, and our CEO, the buyer, was convinced early in the discussion that the service being offered was a good addition to our company. He was ready to buy. The sales person continued with her presentation for another 30 minutes. Consequently, the CEO decided not to buy, because he didn't feel like anyone was listening to his needs. How would the relationship with that company serve his needs in the future? Modeling the behavior of how you will listen and service the customer before, during, and after the sale sends a critical message that builds trust in yourself as a sales person and in your company.

SALES PROFESSIONAL STORY

My dad found the right moment to ask for the sale by searching out his client's real needs for their photos. Did they want to remember themselves in a certain way? Did they want to capture a moment in time? Did they just want a family history? He helped them to define the value that his pictures would bring them. He could then help them, as well as himself, make a business case for his proposal. This was subtle, but intuitive, business acumen. He actually engaged his customer in helping him make that business case. Asking for the order was a natural step in his collaborative process. The customers had defined their own order and were waiting for Dad to finalize it.

Create Sales Professionals

My second sales culture workshop was created in response to the need to create and nurture great sales *professionals*. It is called "Solid Sales Rep and Genius Sales Professional." A great sales professional can carry the sales culture forward because sales professionals are great *business* professionals.

Being a great sales professional does not depend on your title. You can be called a sales rep and still be a sales professional by doing the things that sales professionals do. Being a sales professional does not end with the sales team but envelops *everyone* in some fashion in the sales culture. We all need to understand sales and the role we play. This is accomplished by understanding sales rep skills and sales professional *expertise*. Once you make the commitment to groom sales professionals, you will have better client conversations, better sales campaigns, better sales planning, and great sales results.

Hold People Accountable to the Client

Suggesting that the client comes first does not break any new ground. However, making this a part of the framework is a necessity because the idea of a sales culture is so closely tied to the principle of client centricity. Therefore this step is also one of behavior. Every action and conversation we have relates to the client and has an effect on the sales campaign. Accountability to the client also affects who we invite to join the virtual team, and ultimately affects the transparency of the sales campaign.

Networking Excellence

Do you want to grow your business? Do you want to surpass your competition? Do you want to position your sales culture to succeed by expanding your virtual team? Then make sure that your sales professionals are expert networkers. Every sales professional must be able to network and leverage the power of networking. Here is how to make that happen:

- ❏ Make networking a must and not an option. Create networking accountabilities as a part of the sales professional development.
- ❏ Require every sales professional to identify two organizations or groups that they can attend on a regular

basis, and in which they can take a leadership role and become the "go to" person.

❏ Measure networking activities in every sales meeting and review, the same way you are measuring calls, meetings, and proposals. Don't miss this one—it is a differentiator and can grow your sales culture.

❏ Develop opportunities to present to groups of people so you are seen as the educator and not just the "sales guy" in the room.

❏ Develop a thought leadership platform for each sales team that becomes the value proposition they take to the networking meetings and presentations.

❏ End every networking conversation with "What can I do for you?" Then make sure you follow up!

Hone the Value Proposition

To put power in your networking, the sales teams and the whole virtual team must have a clear and crisp *value proposition*. A value proposition isn't your mission statement, it's a statement of the benefits you can deliver and that your clients can't do without. It is a concise statement that, once uttered by the sales professional, will spark more conversation. This is the acid test of a good value proposition—do you capture someone's imagination?

*To put power in your networking have
a clear and crisp value statement.*

A great sales professional can articulate a value proposition and use it to move campaigns forward. The value proposition can bring people to the virtual team and inspire the clients to see the vision of what you can offer. It doesn't matter whether you are the CEO or the receptionist—everyone is in sales and the value proposition better be consistent across the organization.

People want to do business with people in companies where everyone "gets it" and can be passionate about the value proposition. Ultimately the clients will tell you whether you have the value proposition right. If they buy, that's a good sign. If they don't, you still have work to do!

The value proposition better be
consistent across the organization.

Scalable and Sound Sales Processes

Great sales organizations all have sound and robust sales processes in place. The best sales organizations have sales processes that promote and measure the volume and quality of the business.

Sales process does not happen in a vacuum and it does not suddenly appear. It happens when senior management and sales leadership collaborate and decide what to measure, how to review, and on what basis to review. Take this a step further and include the key members of the other functional areas in the planning and review process. Create the virtual team internally and get involvement in the sales process early on. That may sound shocking, but think of what we have learned about the virtual team and how everyone is in sales!

Establishing a sales process is not terribly daunting, but if you are starting from scratch, here are some pointers:

1. The review process has to be consistent from the top to the bottom. If you are not sure what that means, please go back and review Chapter 4, on sales transparency.

2. Every individual contributor needs to provide at least a weekly plan and review, a quarterly territory review, and an annual territory review. The goal is to understand where the business is coming from and *how* the business will happen.

3. It doesn't matter that you "feel good" about a deal or you "think" you can or that you "assume" something. Tell me *how*. My good friend Mike has always told me "Facts don't lie," and in sales this is true.

4. The sales leader is responsible for making sure the process is followed and sales conversations happen in line with the CRM. All reporting also reflects the data from the CRM.

5. Senior management is accountable to make sure that sales leadership follows the process and is keeping the conversation consistent at all rungs of the ladder.

6. Senior management also sets the expectation that everyone is on virtual teams working together for the company to grow and prosper.

Ultimately, the goal is to have *one consistent sales conversation*. Where everyone is focused on getting the deal closed, everyone understands the big picture. The whole virtual team knows who needs to be involved and when. The sales culture cannot thrive until this happens and happens consistently.

(Sales) Metrics are for Everyone

When the sales culture is in place, then everyone's performance evaluation should include sales culture metrics. Because some people do not directly sign contracts with clients, their performance won't be measured against a dollar amount or the number of sales calls they make. Rather they will be measured against the behaviors described in this book. They will be held accountable for:

- ❏ Serving on a virtual team
- ❏ Accompanying a sales professional on a call
- ❏ Connecting with clients
- ❏ Sharing customer information with the rest of the virtual team
- ❏ Responding to the needs of clients
- ❏ Networking in appropriate community and professional organizations

Hire Passion and Energy

In my sales culture workshop "Essential Selling Skills," we talk about traits and characteristics of great sales professionals. Two of those are passion and energy! Don't hire sales professionals who don't come with these two indispensable elements in abundance. Almost miraculous things happen when sales professionals, or the sales leader, or even the CEO, inspire clients and prospects with their passion for the business and the proposed solution. The power of passion and energy is undeniable and incalculable. It is amazing and so much fun to see it in action. It is so much fun to see the people of the sales culture all get on board with that common passion. You want to build a rock solid virtual team? It's simple—get excited!

The power of passion and energy is undeniable and incalculable.

Create Armies of Proxy Sales Professionals a.k.a. Virtual Teams

Now, think about the elements of the sales culture that we have discussed thus far. When you follow the sales culture framework, you create armies of sales people who are inspired, motivated, and passionate about what you do. They will become your best source of business and referrals. Your virtual teams—both internally and externally—become your strongest and most valuable asset and a huge competitive advantage. This is not a new phenomenon. My dad created armies of sales professionals among his virtual team before the advent of technology like the social networks and databases that make it easy for us to keep in touch with our colleagues.

Discover and Develop Collaborative Relationships

Sounds like a mouthful? Well it's a big thing to do and a bold thing to do. Define areas of common purpose and encourage and expect people to work collaboratively to make the sales culture work. Sales leadership needs to have a close working relationship with every functional area of the business such as the human resources, legal, and finance departments. For example, in order to see the right people hired and build your team of sales professionals, you need help and HR is the place to get it.

I have often asked HR partners to help with the hiring and development process and they became as invested as I was. They became central to my virtual team. We challenged each other. They went on sales calls with sales professionals. And they sometimes asked for help reviewing certain processes.

---

*It takes a partnership with HR to hire
the right people for a sales culture.*

Potential partnerships are all over your company just waiting to be discovered and developed to make the sales culture hum with anticipation and excitement. In your company, is sales connected with marketing? Is product development connected with the client? Senior management and sales leadership must make sure that all areas of the business are participating in all sales conversations, meetings, and campaigns. The process needs to be highly inclusive and collaborative. Break down the silos and invite people to be part of the solution and the sales culture!

What's in It for Us?

In a sales culture the sales professional is always ready to answer questions when he asks someone to be a part of the virtual team. While the answers always focus on the client, answering questions also reflects the ability of the sales professional to *inspire and motivate* others to give their best to satisfy the client. So, what is in it for us? It's the ability to understand how vital each person's contribution is to the sale.

People in a sales culture hold each other accountable! Does this sound familiar? This is a key component that cannot be underestimated. If people say "Well, that's someone else's issue," that doesn't get the task done. The peer who notices an issue that needs to be addressed must communicate with the peer who can make it happen. That's what closes deals.

Peer to peer coaching is mandatory to make sure the sales culture bursts with life and vitality.

Tell Me How

The concept of "How" has come up a couple of times in the sales culture framework. It's time to expand on the nature of the "how"— that's how with a big H, and how with a small H. The big H How in a sales culture is *How to get things done.* Conversations in a sales campaign are focused on the *how* we will make this solution for the client, or the *how* we will get this deal closed and so forth.

The small H how refers to *how we feel* about sales. Without a sales culture environment, far too many sales campaigns and sales conversations start and get mired in how people *feel* about things or how they *assume* something or how they *think* things might play out. Feelings, thoughts, and assumptions don't get the deal done. You need a clear understanding of *How* you will leverage every person and tool at your disposal to complete the steps and actions that will close the deal.

Feeling good and being excited about a sales call or a proposal or a conversation with a client is essential and should be nurtured. However, we can't stop there.

---

*The sales culture rides on the facts of the **How to get things done** and not just how you feel.*

Final Thoughts

Now that you understand the necessary and fundamental components of a sales culture, I want to speak to the various people who are responsible to make this a reality and share some final thoughts with you.

Senior Management

Sales culture starts with you! You have the choice to commit your organization to having a place where you focus on the client and do not operate in a vacuum. I have seen far too many companies and products flame out because they were built and developed by people who had the "If I create it they will come" attitude. There was no collaboration with the prospects and clients and no help or input from the sales organization. People were allowed to operate with impunity in silos and the sales team was responsible to get products sold, and it could not be done. There was no sales culture, no partnership, and hence *no sales.*

The best part from your perspective is that the decision to create a sales culture costs you little or nothing. OK, the CRM is not free, but it is well worth the investment.

Your board will not fire you for deciding against mediocrity! The establishment of a sales culture means a firm and decisive commitment to the principles we have laid out and holding people accountable to the sales culture vocabulary and principles. Don't have sales conversation without asking *How* and don't allow anyone to retreat into the silo of ignorance and bliss.

Sales Leadership

Sales culture starts with you! You are a sales leader. Do you truly know what your number one job is? It is to coach, train, and mentor your people to be successful and to be great sales professionals. Your other job is to create a sales culture in your team. Your job is *not* to close business, but to make sure your people are equipped and motivated to get the job done. Your job is to make sure that the sales culture lives through your people and that you are holding them accountable. If a sales professional comes to the table unprepared to talk about their business, then the conversation does not happen. If conversations do not reflect the CRM, then ask why. If you see a sales professional acting alone, then ask why.

You have a choice. You can insist that your sales teams are doing the right things and are engaging the right people. You can ensure that they are expanding their reach through networking and virtual team building to power up the results! Sales culture is industry neutral. Whether you are a for profit, a nonprofit, or an association; you better "get" that the rules have changed and we all need to engage in selling in some way. If "Sales" is a just five-letter word to you, then you have just chosen mediocrity.

Sales Professionals

Sales culture starts with you! You probably saw that coming, but it's true! If you want to commit yourself to a path of greatness, start with making sure that you are acting in accordance with the principles and ideals of the sales culture. Hold your peers and colleagues accountable to the sales culture. Don't wait to be told what do. Get in front of the issues and in front of the pack. Remember that sales professionals are business people who view their territory as a business and act accordingly. Sales reps take orders. Sales professionals run a business and build a sales culture.

Who is on your virtual team? Who is selling for you? Are you rousing others or are you in a silo? Are you holding yourself accountable or are you pointing the finger at someone else because they did not get something done? Are you networking and inspiring people externally to want to help and work with you and perhaps buy from you? You want to ask yourself these questions, not once but constantly. You also need to hold your manager accountable to you to create a sales culture consistent with yours.

Everyone in the Organization

Sales culture lives through you! You are in sales. Everything you do has an effect on the prospects and the client's prospects and their desire and interest in buying. Don't ever forget that! You play a role in the developing of revenue. Whether your contribution is direct or indirect, spontaneous or systemic; you are the key to the sales culture. Welcome to sales! We want you and need you.

Questions for You to Think About

1. Has everyone in your organization received basic sales training even if they do not have direct sales responsibility?

2. Where are you networking?

3. Are you coaching your virtual team or are you telling them what to do?

4. Are your sales processes understood across the organization?

5. Who on your team is not aware of what is going on in the organization?

6. What is your value proposition?

7. Who is on your virtual team? Can you define your first string, second string, third string?

8. Can everyone on your virtual team inspire with the value proposition?

9. If you have a CRM, does everyone in your organization know how to use the CRM?

10. Are you a sales rep or a sales professional?

11. Do you have an army of proxy sales professionals?

Todd Cohen

Todd Cohen works with business professionals and companies who want to create a high-performance sales culture, helping them meet and exceed their goals and increase their sales. Since 1984, Todd has coached and led sales teams to deliver more than $700 million in revenue for leading companies including Xerox, Gartner Group, Pensare, Thomson-Reuters and LexisNexis.

Todd is a highly sought-after keynote speaker and his Sales Culture Workshops™ have been met with wide acclaim. He is the President of the Philadelphia Chapter of the National Speakers Association for 2012–2013 and he serves as chair of Sales and Marketing group of the Greater Philadelphia Senior Executives Group. Todd is also a regular contributor in the *Philadelphia Business Journal* and he is a passionate networker and connector of sales professionals, entrepreneurs, and executives in transition. Todd is the Sales Executive in Residence at the Innovation and Entrepreneurship Institute (IEI) at Temple University's Fox School of Business, his alma mater.

Todd inspires, advises, and builds high-performance sales teams that produce outstanding results. He also provides strategic oversight for sales teams and serves as executive sales coach and advisor to clients ranging from small, rapidly growing start-ups to large, well-established corporations.

Todd with his dad, Marvin Cohen, 1984

Create Sales Culture Today

YOU can contribute to the overall success of your organization, no matter what your position. **You simply need to think differently about what you do**.

If you are ready to create a high-performance sales culture within your organization and boost your company's sales and increase its market share, Todd is available for:

❏ **Keynotes**: Book Todd to be a keynote speaker at your next company event, association or sales meeting.

❏ **Sales Culture Workshops™**: Hire Todd to bring his interactive workshops to your organization.

❏ **Consulting**: Engage Todd to build a highly-effective sales team for your company and train and mentor your executives on how to maintain a lasting high-performance sales culture.

To engage Todd for your organization
or for volume sales orders of *Everyone's in Sales*,
please call 866–515–9445,
email todd@toddcohen.com,
or visit http://www.toddcohen.com.